The Other Side of the Dark

The Other Side of the Dark

Four Plays by Judith Thompson

*The Crackwalker · Pink
Tornado · I Am Yours*

Coach House Press Toronto

Great North Artists Management Inc., 350 Dupont Street, Toronto, Ontario, Canada M5R 1V9

The punctuation of these plays carefully adheres to the author's instructions.

Published with the assistance of the Canada Council, the Ontario Arts Council, and the Ontario Ministry of Culture and Communications.

Editor for the Press: Robert Wallace

For a list of our other drama titles, or to receive a catalogue, write to The Coach House Press, 401 (rear) Huron Street, Toronto, Canada M5S 2G5   (416) 979-7374.

Photo credits: *The Crackwalker:* Theatre Passe Muraille; *I Am Yours* and back cover: Michael Cooper Photographic.

Cover design: Gordon Robertson.   Text design: Nelson Adams
Printed in Canada at The Coach House Press, Toronto

Canadian Cataloguing in Publication Data
Thompson, Judith, 1954-
The other side of the dark: Four plays by Judith Thompson
Contents: The crackwalker – I am yours – Tornado – Pink.
I SBN 0-88910-378-X
I. Title.
PS8589.H4883O75 1989   C812 '.54   C89-094807-0
PR9199.3.T56O75 1989

I would like to thank
Robert Wallace,
Urjo Kareda,
Gregor Campbell,
Victoria Ridout
and
Michael Ondaatje.

This book is for Ariane.

Contents

Introduction

In the concentrated, accelerated history of contemporary Canadian drama, Judith Thompson's *The Crackwalker* – first produced in 1980 – has achieved its classic status. It is regularly produced, read, studied and imitated. Yet even now, encountering it again, it can still take your breath away with its daring and its power. Its view of lives scratched out on the margins of our society is both unsparing and generous. Judith Thompson hears the poetry of the inarticulate and the semi-literate, embodying the colloquialisms, the brand names, the fractured but expressive syntax, with the urgency of their speakers. She frees her words to carry their wild, unruly, seeking spirits. These characters do terrible things, and they have terrible things done to them. They have no champions, except for their playwright, who in creating them gives them, unequivocally, their moment of self-knowledge, their moment of dignity, their moment of visionary ecstasy.

In the decade since *The Crackwalker,* her first play, Judith Thompson has written two more full-length stage plays, *White Biting Dog* (1984) and *I Am Yours* (1987), a few shorter stage pieces, and several radio plays, television scripts and screenplays. She has broadened her social perspective to include many levels of our world, but she remains always acutely attuned to class tensions. Indeed, *I Am Yours* in many ways is a play about social warfare. She has retained her creative (and personal) obsession with birth and childhood, and a small infant plays a pivotal role in many of her major works: Danny in *The Crackwalker,* Tracy Meg in *I Am Yours,* and Jenny in *Tornado.* The perplexing relationships between parents and children remain a central organizing principle in the deployment of her characters. Few of her works do

not present at least two generations of a bloodline.
Moreover, she also explores the dissonances between
biological mothers and their spiritual, symbolic,
parallel rivals (Lucy's mother and Nellie in *Pink*, Dee
and Pegs in *I Am Yours*, Rose and Amanda in *Tornado*).
Violent behaviour and brutal action sweep
torrentially through her characters' lives; *Tornado*
would be a good title for several of her works (though
each of her chosen titles is memorable). But the most
illuminating and revealing characteristic of Judith
Thompson's work is her profound imaginative
understanding of the naked human creature.
    She is overwhelmingly aware of the physical side of
our biology. Her characters are not spared revelation
of the intimate details of their bodies. Piss, shit, sweat,
blood, saliva, vomit, tears, mucous, semen, amniotic
fluid – these are as central and as inescapable a part of
our beings as our heart, our mind, our soul. Her
characters suffer from a wide range of hungers, a
famished line that pulls together the deep pangs of
sexual hunger to the solace-hunger for sweet, greasy
junk foods. They struggle, they gasp for breath, and
fear that this primal power will be lost. Alan, in *The
Crackwalker*, describes his dying father as 'trying to
find the fucking air'; Mercy, in *I Am Yours*, finds
herself, after her own mother's death, 'startled ... to
hear my own breath ... keep ... on'; and Jake, in the
final moment of *Tornado*, urges Amanda to 'let the
scream take ya let it carry you up bang! through to the
air.'
    The other threat to sustaining life is the animalistic
side within each of us – the darker, unconscious,
libidinous, sometimes destructive, chaotic dream-
world inside, 'the other side of the dark,' as described
in *Tornado*. The fluidity of Judith Thompson's
language, with its free, unexpected rhythms, has
made it possible for her always to suggest the swift,
vibrating oscillation between conscious and
unconscious states. In *I Am Yours*, several early scenes

are described as dreams, and as the characters surrender their hold on their own powers of control, they enter new half-awake, half-dreaming scenes (the haunting reunion of Mercy and Raymond is described in the stage directions as 'perhaps a dream'). But *I Am Yours* is particularly rich and dense with the exploration of 'the animal behind the wall,' or the beast within. Mack describes a six-foot-high honeycomb of 50,000 bees found living behind a wall. Dee describes 'a shark banging at the shark-cage and sliding out' after she has had sex with Toilane (who describes it as 'You showin me ... your animal'); and she describes 'a lion breaking through a wall' when she is going into labour with their child. Harsh attempts to eliminate the animal leave a gaping, searing vacuum: at night, Mack feels 'a burning hole,' just as Sandy in *The Crackwalker* described the violent effects of Joe's love: 'I got a fucking hole in my gut cause of you.' The solution to the throbbing, buzzing honeycomb behind Mack's wall is to 'carve these holes in it.'

The candid, almost giddy non-privacy of her characters is probably one of the things that most excites some audiences about Judith Thompson's work, and also what repels and disturbs some others. She herself really has no choice: her extraordinary strength and intimacy come from the way she works. She *inhabits* her characters – or, as she herself has said, she stands in their blood. She is herself uncommonly attuned to the processes of her physical self; at any given moment, she can provide an account of the state of her various organs. She seems able to track her own circulation. That openness and sensual receptivity extends, too, to the world around her: she observes, absorbs, listens with almost otherworldly intensity to *this* world. Fragments of overheard vernacular will turn up in her dialogue, so that her plays contain collages of the language of modern urban life, polished to a brilliant comic lustre. An image caught

from her window may be developed into a
monologue. A found object will be incorporated,
perhaps as a synthesizing agent (she found the
German poem in *I Am Yours* by accident, at random,
between drafts). She is insistent upon hearing her
characters' individual voices. In manuscript form her
scripts are a mystery of odd spellings, cryptic
punctuation, arrows and drawings – all ways of
notating her people's melodies, their inflections and
rhythms.

For her, the physical, the verbal and the spiritual
are all important, and all simultaneous. She sees and
allows no separation among them. Judith Thompson
could take as her motto the words of one of Tennessee
Williams's characters: 'Nothing human disgusts me.'
Everything is human. Our dreams, our words, our
actions, our orgasms, our shit – everything defines us.
An incident can elicit either wild grief or wilder
laughter (as Alan says of Theresa in *The Crackwalker*,
'ya cry the same way ya laugh'). Because everything is
part of the human spectrum, Judith Thompson
doesn't judge her characters. The animal – the other
side of the dark – they are within us, part of us. She
has a sober acknowledgement of evil, but it is
understood as part of the original sin we all bear. Her
plays contain shocking betrayals (as Mercy betrays
Dee) and exceptional loyalties (as Sandy is loyal to
Theresa), but they are parts of the same impulse.
Mercy admits that she is so afraid of her sister because
she loves her. In the shadows of such paradoxes,
Judith Thompson's characters struggle with their sins,
their self-hatred, their guilt. They grapple with their
animal.

It is this elemental grappling that Judith Thompson
dramatizes, which she invests with her remarkable
resources of invention, understanding and
compassion, the tools which lance, probe and heal the
human struggle. She embraces the possibility of
redemption. Both Toilane and Dee search and beg for

forgiveness in the final scenes of *I Am Yours*, and are rewarded with transfiguration. Bleak, harrowing and frightening as they may be, the movement of Judith Thompson's plays is usually regenerative – from sin toward grace, from the tornado of suffocation to the restoration of breath.

Urjo Kareda, August 1989

Urjo Kareda is the artistic director of Toronto's Tarragon Theatre.

The Crackwalker

Notes

The Crackwalker was first produced by Theatre Passe Muraille, Toronto, in November, 1980, with the following cast:

THERESA JoAnn McIntyre
SANDY Jane Foster
ALAN Hardee T. Lineham
JOE Geza Kovacs
THE MAN Graham Greene

Directed by Clarke Rogers.

Set and costume design: Patsy Lang.

Author's Foreword

I am indebted to Michael Mawson for giving me my first recognition as a playwright. His encouragement and advice gave me confidence as a writer and the much-needed influence of an editor.

I would also like to thank Cameron Wallace and Marc Brisson.

This play is dedicated to the memory of my father.

Act One, Scene One

THERESA Shut up, mouth, I not goin back there no more no way, I'm goin back to Sandy's! [*to audience*] You know what she done to me? She make me go livin with her up on Division near Chung Wah's, cause she say I come from God, eh, then she go lookin in my room every night see if I got guys in there cause Bonnie Cain told her I was suckin off queers down the Lido for five bucks; I wasn't doin it anyways Bonnie Cain was doin it I was just watchin. So last night, eh, I'm up there with a friend of mine, Danny, he a taxi driver – we're just talkin, eh, we weren't doin nothin, and so she come up and knock on the door and she say, 'Trese I know you got someone in there' and I go 'No Mrs. Beddison ain't nobody in here,' and she start goin on about God and that, and how she knowed cause she got a six feelin in her, so I get scared, eh, so I tell Danny to get in the closet. We don't got no clothes on, eh, so I put his jeans and that under the covers like I'm sleepin and I go 'S'kay Mrs. Beddison you could come in now.' So she come in lookin at me like a stupid bitch and she say she knowed there was somebody in there cause she heard talkin and I says 'You feelin okay Mrs. Beddison, ain't nobody here cept me and I sleepin,' then she start goin near the closet, eh, and Danny start laughin. Well she runup the closet and she pullin on the door and I'm pullin on her arm and I'm saying 'Trust me Mrs. Beddison, ya gotta trus me,' cause the sosha workers are always goin on about trus and that, eh, but she don't listen, she open the door and there's Danny standin stripped naked. Well that whoredog Beddison start screamin God words at him, eh, so he takes off outa the house and she takes off after him and I got his pants, eh, so I throw em out the window case he catch em and then I bawlin. I bawlin on the bed and ya know what she make me do? She make me take a bath! A bubble bath like for the baby! All bubbles and that! Then she make me put on her stupid dressin robe itch my skin and smell like chocolate bars and that and she take me to where she livin and you know what she make me do? She make me read the Bible! I don't like readin no stupid Bible! Ya get a stomach ache doin that, ya do! Stupid hose bag. I'm not goin back there no more no way, I'm goin back to Sandy's.

Act One, Scene Two

SANDY *and* JOE's *apartment.* SANDY *is scrubbing the floor furiously.* THERESA *appears, joyous, carrying a plastic bag containing all of her belongings. As she has not seen* SANDY *in several weeks, she is very excited.*

THERESA   Hi Sandy, how ya doin!!
          [SANDY *does not look at* THERESA]
SANDY   What are you doin here?
THERESA   I come callin on ya!
          [*In the following sequence,* SANDY's *anger builds. At first, however, it contains an element of teasing*]
SANDY   I don't want no houndogs callin on me. [*continues scrubbing*]
THERESA   I not a houndog!
SANDY   Yes, y'are.
THERESA   No I not.
SANDY   Whoredog houndog that's what you are.
THERESA   [*laughs, delighted*] Sanny!
SANDY   [*pointing backwards*] And get your whorepaws offa my sofa.
THERESA   [*jumps, removes hand, gasps*] Sanny, like I don't mean to bug ya or nothin [*eating doughnut from bag*] but like I don't get off on livin where I'm livin no more so I come back here sleepin on the couch, okay?
SANDY   I not keepin no cowpies here.
THERESA   I not a cowpie!
SANDY   [*faces her*] Would you get out of my house?
THERESA   Why, what I done?

SANDY ... Ya smell like cookin fat – turns my gut.

THERESA That only cause I eatin chip from the chipwagon!

SANDY I don't care what it's cause of, get your whoreface out of here.

THERESA Why, why you bein ugly for?

SANDY You tell me and then we'll both know.

THERESA What.

SANDY Don't think nobody seen ya neither cause Bonnie Cain seen ya right through the picture window!
[THERESA *claps a hand to her mouth s in 'uh-oh'*]
On my couch that I paid for with my money.

THERESA Wha –

SANDY With *my husband!*

THERESA No way, Sanny.

SANDY [*unable to contain her anger any longer*] You touch my fuckin husband again and I break every bone in your body!

THERESA Bonnie Cain lyin she lyin to ya she think I took twenty buck off her she tryin to get me back.

SANDY [*starts speaking after 'she lying to ya'*] That's bullshit Therese cause Bonnie Cain don't lie and you know she don't.

THERESA You don't trus me.

SANDY Fuckin right.

THERESA I never done it.

SANDY Pretty bad combination, Trese, a retarded whore.

THERESA That's a load of bullshit Sanny, I *not retarded.*

SANDY Just get out of my house and don't come back. [*pushes her*]

THERESA No I *never* I never done it! [*in angry indignation she pushes back*]

SANDY Trese Joe told me, he told me what the two of youse done!

THERESA Oh.

SANDY Lyin whore, look at ya make me sick. Wearin that ugly dress thinkin it's sexy cause it shows off your fat tits and those shoes are fuckin stupid ya can't even walk in them.

THERESA I know.

[SANDY *stares at* THERESA. THERESA *does not move*]

SANDY [*with an air of resignation, tiredness*] Just get out, okay?

THERESA I never wanted it, Sanny, I never wanted it he come in he made me.

SANDY Bull Trese.

THERESA He did I sleepin I sleepin there havin dreams I seen this puppy and he come in and tie me up and push it in me down my hole.

SANDY What?

THERESA He tie me all up with strings and that and he singin Ol Macdonel Farm and he say he gonna kill me if I don't shut up so I be quiet and he done it he screw me.

SANDY Are you shittin me?

THERESA And – and – and he singin and he take his jean down and it all hard and smellin like pee pee and he go and he put it in my mouth.

SANDY He could do twenty for that.

THERESA Don't send him up the river Sanny he didn't mean nothin.

SANDY Horny bastard he's not gettin into me again.

THERESA Me neither Sanny he tries anything I just run up to Tom Horton's get a fancy doughnut.

SANDY Oh he won't be cheatin on me again.

THERESA How come Sanny, you tell him off?

SANDY Fuckin right I did. After Bonnie tole me, I start givin him shit, eh, and he takes the hand to me callin me a hag and sayin how he liked pokin you better'n that and look. [*reveals bruise*]

THERESA Bassard.

SANDY He's done it before, but he won't do it again.

THERESA Why, Sanny, you call the cops on him?

SANDY *Right.*

THERESA Did ya –

SANDY Ya know my high heels? The shiny black ones I got up in Toronto?

THERESA Yeah, they're sharp.

SANDY [*obviously enjoying telling the story*] And he knows it, too. After he beat up on me he takes off drinkin, comes back about three just shitfaced, eh, and passes out cold? Well I'm there lookin at him snorin like a pig and I says to myself 'I'm gonna get this bastard.' I'm thinkin of how when I seen my heels sittin over in the corner and then I know what I'm gonna do. So I take one of the heels and go over real quiet to where he's lyin, and ya know what I do? I take the heel and I rip the holy shit out of his back with it.

THERESA JEEZ DID HE WAKE UP?

SANDY Fuckin right he did. You shoulda seen him, first I guess he thought he was dreamin, eh, so he just lies there makin these ugly noises burpin and that? And then he opens his eyes, and puts his hands up like a baby eh, and *then* I *seen* him *see* the heel. Well I take off right out the back door and he's comin after me fit to kill his eyes is all red he's hissin I am scared shitless; well he gets ahold of me and I says to myself 'Sandy this is it. This is how you're gonna die. You got the bastard back and now you're gonna die for it.' Well he is just about to send me to the fuckin angels when he stops; just like that and turns around and goes on to bed.

THERESA How come he done that, Sanny?

SANDY I didn't know at first either, then I figured it out. Cuttin him with the heel was the smartest thing I done. Ya see, he wasn't gonna kill me cause he don't want to do time, eh, and he knew if he just beat up on me he'd never get no more sleep cause I'd do it again. He knows it. He don't dare take a hand to me again, no way. Either he takes off, or he stays and he treats me nice.

THERESA Did you talk to him later?

SANDY I ain't seen him for three days. But we ate together before he took off, I fixed him up some tuna casserole and we ate it; we didn't say nothin, though. It don't matter, we sometimes go a whole week without talkin, don't mean we're pissed off at each other.

THERESA Al and I talkin all the time when we go out.

SANDY We did too when we first started goin together. After a while ya don't have to talk cause you always know what they're gonna say anyways. Makes ya sick sometimes. What are you bawlin for?

THERESA I'm sorry Joe done that to me, Sanny.

SANDY   He's like that, he's a prick.
THERESA S'okay if I come livin here then?
SANDY   ... Sure, I don't care.
THERESA Thank you Sanny.
SANDY   I like the company.
THERESA Don't say nothin to Al, eh?
SANDY   What if I tell him what Bonnie Cain tole me about you
         blowin off queers down the Lido?
THERESA Oh no, Sanny, don't say bout that.
SANDY   I guess old fags in Kingston are pretty hard up.
THERESA You want a doughnut, Sanny?
SANDY   No. What kind ya got.
THERESA Apple fritters.
SANDY   Jeez, Therese, ya ever see how they make them things?
THERESA No, I never worked up there.
SANDY   It'd make ya sick.
THERESA I love em.
SANDY   I know ya do, you're a pig.
THERESA Fuck off.... Only kiddin.
SANDY   You watch your mouth.
THERESA You love Joe still?
SANDY   I don't know. I used to feel like we was in the fuckin
         movies. Member that show *Funny Girl* where Barbara
         Streisand and Omar Sharif are goin together?
THERESA She hardly sing pretty.
SANDY   Well remember that part where they start singin right
         on the boat, singin to each other?
THERESA Yeah.
SANDY   We done that once. We'd been up at the Manor, eh,
         Chesty Morgan was up there so we'd just been havin a
         hoot, eh, and Joe wants to go over to the General
         Wolfe to see the Mayor, so we get on the Wolfe Island
         ferry and we're laughin and carryin on and that and
         then we start singin, right on the bow of the Wolfe
         Island ferry.
THERESA Jeez.
SANDY   We didn't care when we were doin it though, we
         didn't give a shit what anyone was thinkin, fuck em
         we were havin fun.

THERESA I love singin.

SANDY Joe really done that to you?

THERESA What?

SANDY *Raped* ya.

THERESA Don't like talkin about it Sanny.

SANDY *Trese.*

THERESA He done it when I never wanted it it's true.

SANDY It is, eh?

THERESA S'true, Sanny. Don't tell Joe, eh?

SANDY I mighta known it.

THERESA Still okay if I sleepin here though?

SANDY You're gonna have to do the housework while I'm working for Nikos.

THERESA How come you workin down there I thought you didn't like Nikos?

SANDY I get off on cornbeef on rye, arswipe, what d'ya think I need the fuckin money.

THERESA Ain't Joe drivin for Amey's no more?

SANDY No.

THERESA What's he doin?

SANDY Fuckin the dog, I don't know.

THERESA Bassard.

SANDY I know. Gimme a bite of that.

THERESA I not really retarded am I Sanny?

SANDY Just a little slow.

THERESA Not like that guy walkin downstreet lookin at the sidewalk?

SANDY Jeez he give me the creeps.

THERESA He hardly got the long beard, eh?

SANDY I know.

THERESA Not like him, eh Sanny?

SANDY No. No, I tole ya Therese, you're just a little slow.

THERESA Oh.

[JOE and ALAN *barge in with a hot motorbike. They start quickly, efficiently taking it apart and packing the parts.* SANDY *and* THERESA *stand there stupefied*]

JOE Ya hoo! We got ourselves a shit hot mother!

ALAN Did we *ever!*

JOE Okay nice and easy we don't want to mark this babe.

ALAN   Like this?

JOE   That's right buddy – fuckin back door wide open shit that dog just sittin there waggin its tail at us.

ALAN   He wanted to be buddies with us.

JOE   I just about shit it was fuckin *helpin* us.

THERESA   What kinda dog was it Al one of them golden?

JOE   A shepherd.

ALAN   A German shepherd a police dog.

JOE   A fuckin *screw* dog.

SANDY   You're not bringin Martin over here.

JOE   How's my pussycake doin? Eh? [*kisses* SANDY] Eh pussycake?

SANDY   I says you're not bringin Martin over here.

JOE   Don't worry babe we're meetin him overto the Shamrock he ain't comin here.

ALAN   Down the Beachcomber Room.

THERESA   That's hardly nice down there all them trees and that?

ALAN   You like it there?

THERESA   I love it.

ALAN   I'll take ya there sometime.

SANDY   Where you been the last three nights?

JOE   Paintin the town brown honeysuck whata you been doin?

SANDY   I said where were ya for three nights in a row?

JOE   Out with the Mayor, poochie, spookin out the Royal.

THERESA   You not out with him he dead.

ALAN   Theresa.

THERESA   He is dead.

ALAN   Joe's only kiddin, Trese.

SANDY   You tell me where ya been or you're out on your ear. I said where were ya the last three nights?

JOE   Just hold on to your pants sugar crack first things first. [*madly working on the bike*]

ALAN   This is big bucks ya know.

SANDY   You don't have to tell me cause I know. I know where ya were you were down the Embassy pissin our money away.

THERESA   Them ugly old Greeks down there anyways.

ALAN   You were takin Papa's *shirt*, eh Joe?

SANDY I'll tell ya somethin about gamblers youse do it just so's you could lose it's true that's why.

JOE Well fuck me blind I never knew that. Did you know that Al?

ALAN Nope, I never heard of that.

JOE That's pretty good commander, where'd ya get that offa?

SANDY It happened to be in *The Reader's Digest*, arswipe, and it was written by a doctor, Doctor John Grant, and I guess he knows what he's talkin about.

JOE Ooooh *Reader's Digest*, shit-for-brains is going smart on us.

THERESA She not a shit-for-brains you stupid.

JOE You simmer down there burger.

SANDY Is that where ya were, pissin away my money?

JOE [*completes a physical action*] Gotcha.

SANDY Eh?

JOE Hand me the pliers, would ya?

SANDY [*screeching*] I said where were ya Joe!

[JOE *spits his mouthful of beer in her face.* ALAN *laughs and laughs*]

SANDY That's cute.

THERESA Stupid dummy-face.

[JOE *spits on* ALAN. ALAN *laughs, spits back*]

SANDY You are cut off and I mean it.

JOE From what, bitch, your ugly box?

[SANDY *exits to clean up*]

JOE Don't know what she's so pissed off at nice brew in the face cool ya right down.

THERESA I'm movin back here Joe Sanny said I could.

ALAN She did?

JOE Is that right.

THERESA Sleepin on the couch that okay Joe?

JOE Sure, fuck, I don't care, long as the two of youse don't gang up on me.

ALAN Two women together always do.

THERESA What do two women do?

ALAN You know, gang up on the guy.

SANDY [*entering*] Only if he got it comin to him.

JOE Do I get it comin to me commander?

SANDY You're fuckin right you do.

JOE Little diesel dyke this one see what she done to me?

ALAN Holy Jeez!

JOE She's a live one all right Pearl Lasalle the second.

THERESA She not like Pearl Lasalle Pearl Lasalle ugly lookin.

JOE She fights like her though don't ya honey suck? What's for supper I'm starvin.

SANDY Nothin.

JOE What?

SANDY You don't bring in money we don't get no supper.

JOE Well fuck – don't we got stuff for samiches?

SANDY Nope.

JOE Well fuck I'm goin over to Shirley's.

SANDY When.

JOE Right now fuck.

SANDY Take your stuff with ya.

JOE Would ya sit on this first I want fish for supper.

SANDY Pig. I says take your stuff with ya and get out.

JOE You for real?

SANDY Fuckin right.

JOE All right I been wantin out of this hole. Thanks babe.

SANDY Is that right?

JOE Take care. [*starts to go*]

SANDY You could get in a lot of trouble rapin a retard Joe.

JOE Pardon.

SANDY I said you could get in a lot of trouble rapin a retard.
[THERESA *is motioning 'No! No! No!' to* SANDY]

JOE Yeah that's right you would. So?

SANDY You'll be up the river for twenty years when I tell the cops what you done, Joe.

ALAN Over fifty don't get you twenty years no way no way!

SANDY I'm not talkin bout the bike.

JOE What? What are ya talkin about eh?

SANDY About rapin a retard.

JOE What?

SANDY About rapin Theresa.

JOE What.

SANDY About rapin Theresa with me in the next room.

JOE Rape? Rape? Who told you that did Theresa tell you that.

SANDY Yeahhh.

THERESA No no Sanny not rape I only said he done it when I never wanted it.

JOE Did you tell my wife that I raped you Theresa?
[THERESA *doesn't answer*]
Did you say that? Eh? [*grabs her*] Eh?

THERESA I never – leave me alone you big ugly cock –

JOE I'll tell you somethin about your little girfriend buddy. I'll tell you something about this little –

ALAN It don't matter, Joe, it – it – it just don't matter nobody don't believe her anyways.

JOE This little girl who's callin rape was sittin on that couch beggin for it.

ALAN She never.

SANDY Theresa?

JOE It's true. I come in piss drunk I'm passed out on the floor and there she is down on all fours shovin her big white ass in my face.

THERESA No I never.

JOE Big white bootie right in the face.

THERESA Go away.

JOE Tell em like it was Trese, and no crossin fingers.

THERESA I never say that Sanny, I never mean he rape me!

SANDY Theresa is he tellin the truth?

ALAN Theresa you never done that, did ya? Shown him your bum?

JOE This is your last chance, burger, now tell the fuckin truth or I get serious.

SANDY Don't lie to me Theresa. I can forgive a lot of things but not a lie.

ALAN You can tell the truth, Theresa, I'll take care of ya.

SANDY Eh, Trese?
[*Pause*]

THERESA [*laughing*] Who farted?

ALAN I never did.

JOE Eh Theresa?

ALAN It's – it's okay, Joe it's – she – she can't handle her booze yet she was probably drunk or sniffin and you was drunk and it don't matter, it just don't matter I'll be stayin with her all the nights from now I'm gonna take care of her it won't happen again she won't never say nothin bout ya again I promise.

THERESA You stayin with me all nights from now Al?

ALAN I'm takin care of ya. I'm –

SANDY Could youse leave us alone, please.

ALAN Who, me and Theresa?

SANDY If you don't mind.

ALAN Sure, sure. We –

THERESA Wait for me Al I wanna get some chocolate bars and that I starvin ... well I am I didn't have no dinner.

JOE You. You watch your mouth, eh?

SANDY Would youse just take off?

[ALAN *pulls* THERESA *out*]

THERESA See youse later don't do nothin I wouldn't do.

Act One, Scene Three

ALAN *and* THERESA *exit.* JOE *is furious and trying to cool down. His back is to* SANDY. *She is aware of his anger. She picks something up off the kitchen floor and starts to take it in to the kitchen.* JOE *grabs her as she tries to pass him and throws her to the floor.*

JOE You CUNT.

SANDY Keep away from me –

JOE I'm a fuckin *rapist cause a fuckin retard SAYS so?*

SANDY Touch me again and you go to your goddamn grave!

JOE FUCK maybe I'm the maniac been carvin all the TELLERS out in SASKATOON! [*makes monster face and noise*]

SANDY Go jump in a hole.

JOE [*grabs her, hard*] What is fuckin with your BRAIN, woman?

SANDY I didn't mean it.

JOE It was a *joke?*

SANDY I was just – you said you liked her better.

JOE What?

SANDY You said you liked – pokin her better.

JOE [*laughs, almost hysterically*] So I go to the joint.

SANDY I wasn't gonna tell nobody –

JOE You're a fuckin CROW, you know that?

SANDY I was just – seein –

JOE [*thrusting her away*] Get away from me.

[SANDY *starts to run toward him, trying to scream but the sound is muffled and distorted by a stomach seizure which stops her about three feet away from* JOE]

JOE You got your upset stomach again?

SANDY Bastard.

JOE [*looks her up and down*] You just give me a hard on.

[SANDY *spits on him*]

JOE Hewww you like it when I'm rough with ya, don't ya? Eh? [*moves her roughly, whispers*] Makes your nips stand up when I'm rough with ya.

[SANDY's *hands are still raised.* SANDY *and* JOE *are a foot apart throughout the interchange.* SANDY *looks at him with hatred*]

What, you don't want it? Okay, see ya later! [*he starts to leave*]

SANDY [*head down*] Joe.

JOE What can I do for ya?

[SANDY *smiles*]

Oh, ya *do* want it. Okay, why – why – don't ya take that blouse there off?

[*She removes her blouse*]

Hm. And the skirt.

[*She removes her skirt. She is left in a bra and pantyhose with a low crotch. He nods, looking her up and down*]

How come ya like it like this? Eh? [*shakes his head*] I gotta be somewhere.

[JOE *exits.* SANDY *remains onstage, not moving. Lights out quickly.*]

Act One, Scene Four

THERESA *and* ALAN *are in a restaurant.*

THERESA Where d'ya think Joe took off to?

ALAN I don't know probably drinkin, maybe the Shamrock.

THERESA You think they're splitting up?

ALAN I hope not.

THERESA Me too. I love Sandy, she my best girlfriend.

ALAN I – Joe – he and me are good buddies, too. They go good together anyways.

THERESA Could I have a doughnut?

ALAN What kind, chocolate? I know you like chocolate.

THERESA I love it.

ALAN Sandy's nuts, you're not fat.

THERESA Don't say nothin about it.

ALAN You're not.

THERESA I don't like talkin about it.

ALAN Here. Two chocolate doughnuts.

THERESA Thank you Alan.

ALAN Jesus you're a good lookin girl. You're the prettiest lookin girl I seen.

THERESA Don't talk like that.

ALAN I love screwin with ya. Do you like it with me?

THERESA I don't know – don't ask me that stuff dummy-face.

ALAN I like eatin ya out ya know.

THERESA Shut your mouth people are lookin don't talk like that stupid-face.

ALAN Nobody's lookin. Jeez you're pretty. Just like a little angel. Huh. Like a – I know. I know. I'm gonna call you my little angel from now on. People gonna see ya and they're gonna go 'There's Trese, she's Al's angel.'

THERESA Who gonna say them things?

ALAN Anybody.

THERESA They are?

ALAN Yup.

THERESA You're a dummy-face.

ALAN So beautiful.

THERESA Stop it Al you make me embarrass.

ALAN You're – I was always hopin for someone like you – always happy always laughin and that.

THERESA I cryin sometimes ya know.

ALAN Yeah but ya cry the same way ya laugh. There's somethin – I don't know – as soon as I seen ya I knew I wanted ya. I wanted to marry ya when I seen ya.

THERESA When, when did you say that?

ALAN I never said nothin, I just thought it, all the time.

THERESA We only been goin together for a little while, you know.

ALAN Let's get married.

THERESA Al stop lookin at me like that you embarrassin me.

ALAN Sorry. Did you hear me?

THERESA Yeah. Okay.

ALAN When.

THERESA Tuesday. I ask my sosha worker to come.

ALAN No. Just Joe and me and you and Sandy. Just the four of us. I want Joe to be my best man.

THERESA Sandy could be the flower girl. Uh. Oh.

ALAN What?

THERESA Hope you don't want no babies.

ALAN Why. I do! I do want babies! I get on with babies good!

THERESA Not sposda have none.

ALAN How come? Who told you that?

THERESA The sosha worker, she say I gotta get my tubes tied.

ALAN What's that?

THERESA Operation up the hospital. They tie it up down there so ya won't go havin babies.

ALAN They can't do that to you no way!

THERESA I know they can't but they're doin it.

ALAN They don't have no *right*.

THERESA Yah they do Al I slow.

ALAN Slow? I don't think you're slow who told you that?

THERESA I ain't a good mum Al I can't help it.

ALAN Who said you ain't a good mum?

THERESA All of them just cause when I took off on Dawn.

ALAN Who's Dawn?

THERESA The baby, the other baby.

ALAN You never had a baby before did ya? Did ya?

THERESA Las –

ALAN You didn't have no other man's baby did ya? With another guy?

[*Pause*]

THERESA No, it's Bernice's.

ALAN Who's Bernice?

THERESA My cousin my mum's sister.

ALAN Well how come you were lookin after her baby?

THERESA Cause she was sick up in hospital. Jeez Al.

ALAN Well – what happened what'dja do wrong?

THERESA Nothin it wasn't my fault just one Friday night I was sniffin, eh, so I took off down to the plaza and I leave the baby up the room, eh, I thought I was comin right back, and I met this guy and he buyin me drinks and that then I never knew what happened and I woke up and I asked somebody where I was and I was in Ottawa!

ALAN He took you all the way up to Ottawa? That bastard.

THERESA I never seen him again I thumbed back to Kingston. [crying] I come back to the house and the baby's gone she ain't there so I bawlin I goin everywhere yellin after her and never found nothin then I see Bonnie Cain and she told me they took her up the Children's Aid she dead. So I go on up the Aid and they say she ain't dead she live but they not givin her back cause I unfit.

ALAN Jeez.

THERESA I ain't no more Al I don't sniff or nothin.

ALAN Them bastards.

THERESA Honest.

ALAN I know. I know ya don't and we're gonna have a baby and nobody ain't gonna stop us. We're gonna have our own little baby between you and me and nobody can't say nothin bout it. You're not goin to no hospital, understand?

THERESA But Al she say she gonna cut off my pension check if I don't get my tubes tied.

ALAN Fuck the pension check you're not goin to no hospital.

THERESA Okay Al.

ALAN Come here. You're not goin to no hospital.

THERESA You won't let em do nothin to me, will ya Al?

ALAN Nope. You're my angel and they ain't gonna touch you.... Hey! I know what ya look like now!

THERESA What, a angel?

ALAN That – that madonna lady; you know them pictures they got up in classrooms when you're a kid? Them pictures of the madonna?

THERESA The Virgin Mary?

ALAN Yeah. Her.

THERESA I love her I askin her for stuff.

ALAN Yuh look just like her. Just like the madonna. Cept the madonna picture got a baby in it.

THERESA It do?

ALAN She's holdin it right in her arms. You too, maybe, eh? Eh? Hey! Let's go up to the Good Thief.

THERESA Al I don't know you goin to church! You goin every Sunday?

ALAN No I never went since I was five I just want to go now. We'll go and we'll – we'll like have a party lightin candles and that a party for gettin married!

THERESA I love lightin candles.

ALAN Maybe the Father's gonna be there. They're always happy when someone's gettin married we could tell him!

THERESA Al I gettin sleepy.

ALAN Well after we party I'm gonna put ya right down to sleep over at Joe's. I won't try nothin or nothin.

THERESA What if Sandy be piss off.

ALAN No Trese, they said we could stay there together. The two of us. And we're gonna.

THERESA Okay ... really I lookin like that madonna?

ALAN Just like her. Just like her.

[*He is rocking her in his arms. Lights fade.*]

Act One, Scene Five

JOE Me and the Mayor we'd pick up a couple steak hoagies, and a case of twenty-four, head up to Merton on the hogs – catch some shit group – you know, Mad Dog Fagin, Grapes of Wrath, somethin, get shitfaced then go back to Kingston, pick us up some juicy pie down at Lino's or Horny Tim's, drive it out to middle road, fuck it blind, and have em home by one o'clock. Then we'd go down and catch the last ferry to the island and fuckin ride from one end to the other all fuckin night. Seven o'clock we'd go into Lou's have us some home fries and a couple eggs easy over then head on back to work in Kingston. That was when I was drivin a cat makin a shitload of money just a shitload. Huh – the Mayor was fuckin crazy wasn't nothin he wouldn't do nothin he was smart too he went to university in the States even, he just didn't give a shit about it, you know? He had about a hundred books I seen em all filled with words that long [*measures two feet*] he knew what they meant, too, every one of them but he never let on, ya know? He never let on he knew so much ... we never *talked* about shit, it was the shit we done together made us good buddies. Just doin stuff with a guy you know you're thinkin the same. Anybody touched him I woulda killed them and same goes for him ... he was a damn good driver too but he wasn't *drivin*, Martin was. Fuckin Martin fuckin stoned on STP. Martin – Martin wasn't an asshole, but he stupid you know? Jeez he was stupid. So this Friday night we'd all gotten pissed up the Manor, eh, then we all went over to the island just to fuck around and to see the Mayor's sister, Linda, who was workin at the General Wolfe waitin on tables. So Bart, that was his real name, Bart and me and Martin had all got these new boots over at the A1 men's store really nice you know, all leather, real solid a hundred bucks a pair so we wanted to show em off to Linda, you know, bug her. So Bart gets in there and he's jumpin on tables, eatin all the limes and cherries and that for the drinks singin some gross song about his love boots, he called them. Fuck it was funny – we were killin ourselves but Linda she wasn't laughin her boss was gettin pissed off so she told Bart, she goes 'Bart, get the fuck out of here I think your goddamn boots are shit.' That's what she said. So he give her a big kiss right in front of her boss and we take off in Martin's car. Me and the Mayor in the backseat, Martin and his girlfriend in the front. Well we're headin down the road goin south it's dark but it ain't wet and the last thing I remember Bart looks at me and he says 'I wonder what it's like to fuck an angel' and *bang* everything goes fuckin black. When I come to I'm in the fucking ambulance goin across to Kingston and Bart's lyin there beside me dead only I didn't know it and there's his sister Linda right there in the ambulance. I don't know how she got there – she's all red all black under her eyes and that and she's bawlin just bawlin up a storm and she's huggin his legs and she's sayin something only I can't make out what she's sayin I can't make it out I was so out of it I'm thinkin I'm gonna die I'm thinkin I'm gonna die if I don't make out what she's sayin so I kept tryin to make it out and she kept sayin it and then I knew what she was sayin and you know what it was? ... She was sayin she did like his boots. 'I do like your boots Bart I do like your boots Bart I do like your boots I do like your fuckin boots I do like your boots I do like your boots I do like your boots.' ... She wouldn't fuckin stop it.

Act One, Scene Six

ALAN *and* THERESA *are sound asleep. The room is sometimes lit by passing cars. Noise of people on the street.* THERESA's *steady breathing. Suddenly we hear* JOE, *very drunk, half singing. As soon as* ALAN *hears him he springs into his jeans, legs shaking, and awkwardly tries to light a cigarette. His heart is racing.* JOE *enters.*

ALAN Hey Joe.

JOE Jeeeeeeezus you gimme a scare what are you doin here?

ALAN Stayin with Trese member? Member ya said I could? The – the mum's got company – in from Windsor.

JOE *Windsor.* What a fuckin hole.

ALAN Yeah it's hot down there – in the summer –

JOE Look what I found in the fuckin hallway. Cheese samich with a bloody kleenex stuck to it.
[*This makes* ALAN *very sick*]

ALAN Jeezus who put it there.

JOE I was thinkin maybe the wife left out a little snack for me. Ya want some? Blood'n Cheez Whiz samich? Hey hey hey it's hardly good.

ALAN Hey no – no – no thank you. No way.

JOE What, you don't like eatin blood or somethin?

ALAN I never tried it.

JOE Were you screwin that?

ALAN No! No I mean no I was just I –

JOE Why the hell not?

ALAN Oh no I mean I was eh, like I was a couple hours ago, but not right before ya came in I wasn't.

JOE Jeez you're strange. How come ya got dressed you goin out?

ALAN No – no I'm not goin out – I – I couldn't fuckin sleep, you know? Ya know what that's like? Ya just keep turnin and can't lie right? So I thought I'd wait up and just shoot the shit with you when ya came in.

JOE Strange-o.

ALAN I guess so. Did-dju play tonight?

JOE Papadapa dies!

ALAN He – he was cheatin again?

JOE Fuckin right he was.

ALAN He dies.

JOE Greasy fuck. Fuck once I seen Edwards get him in a half Nelson an he was so greasy he slipped out!

ALAN Ewwww.

JOE Slipped right out. Slimy bastard right in the middle of the game I turn to him and I says 'Papa' I says, 'Don't fuck with me, just don't fuck with me.'

ALAN That's hardly good. Huh. What did he say?

JOE Nothin. He just made one of them noises.

ALAN What, what the ones with their mouth like this? Like a chicken does?

JOE Hah. Yeah it is kinda like a chicken. Gives me the creeps.

ALAN Yeah. Yeah, they do that all the time and the one I worked for, Andy? He *stunk* too, he smelled like matches, you know? After ya light a match?

JOE He's gettin it.

ALAN Yeah?? Yeah? Who's gonna give it to him, are you? Are you gonna give it to him Joe? I'll help ya I hate the bastard. I hate him.

JOE Buddy I am pleadin the Fifth. Fuuuck. [*singing*] 'I gotta get outtaaa this place if it's the lassst ...'

ALAN I know what ya mean, Joe. Too – too – too bad there weren't no late movie on or something – hah – Mr. Ed or somethin.

JOE Who's he when he's at home?

ALAN Mr. Ed? The talkin horse, don't ya remember? 'A horse is a horse of course of course and no one ...'

JOE Hey [*indicating bedroom*] w'she bawlin or did she go out?

ALAN Sleepin when we come in I think.

JOE She's a good woman buddy.

ALAN I know she is Joe. So's Trese.

JOE Are you sure, buddy?

ALAN Oh – that was – she – she didn't mean nothin honest Joe she she just don't think sometimes, ya know?

JOE That mouth of hers is gonna send her up shit creek one day ain't it burger?

ALAN You – you want a smoke?

JOE Whaddya got – menthol, fuck, I can't smoke that shit.

ALAN I know – I didn't buy em a guy a guy give em to me.

JOE Hey hamburger sorry for wakin ya.

THERESA I not a hamburger.

JOE Ooooh I thought ya was!

THERESA You shut up I sleepin.

JOE Okay burger queen. Yeah. Yeah buddy she's okay too.

ALAN Thank you, Joe. So's Sandy.

JOE She never fucked around on me, you know.

ALAN No?

JOE Not once. [*goes to window and leans out*] What a fuckin hole this is eh? ... K fuckin O. [*yells out window*] Fuuuuuuuck.

[SANDY *enters*]

SANDY Would you shut it?

JOE [*singing*] 'I gotta get out of this place.'

SANDY Why don't ya then ya big pig?

JOE I told ya woman don't go callin me pig in public. Jeez she got an ugly mouth, eh?

SANDY You're shitfaced, Joe, go on and pass out.

JOE You make me wanta piss my pants.

SANDY Just go on makin a fool of yourself.

JOE Down woman, me and my pal Al is gonna head up to Horny Tim's and we're gonna pick us up some taileroonie! Then we're gonna go on over to the quarry and we're gonna get ourselves sucked and fucked –

SANDY You're not proud, are ya.

[JOE *bumps into something, falls.* SANDY *starts to pick him up*]

JOE You never fooled around on me, did ya?

SANDY Nope. I never ... did.

JOE [*sings*] 'She's a hooo-o-o-o-nky tonk womannnn gimme [*goes to bedroom*] gimme gimme the [*fading*] honky tonk wom....'
[ALAN *goes to the window and silently mouths 'Fuuuuck,' in imitation of* JOE. *He turns on TV, crouches on sofa, and sings softly, but can't remember the whole song*]

ALAN Nobody – nobody here – but us chickens, nobody here but us guys don't – don't bother me we got work – to do we got stuff to do and eggs to lay – we're busy – chickens – [ALAN *pretends to be a car, makes sounds, mimes a steering wheel*] Neeowwwwwwwwwwww. Whaaaaaa. Fhrhuuummmm. Atta girl.

Act One, Scene Seven

Later, SANDY *brings in bedding to sleep on sofa, turns on lamp, turns off TV, lights cigarette, sits on sofa.*

SANDY He pukes all over the fuckin bed.

ALAN Oooh shit.

SANDY Funny.

ALAN I'm – I'm sorry Sandy I didn't mean to laugh at ya.

SANDY Can I ask you a personal question?

ALAN Yeah, yeah sure – what?

SANDY Am I gettin ugly lookin?

ALAN What?

SANDY You know, mean lookin, uglier lookin.

ALAN Shit no, jeez – you – you look nice I think ya do! Who, who said that?

SANDY No one. Are ya sure?

ALAN Sure, sure I am you're a good looker I even heard people say ya was.

SANDY Who, who said that?

ALAN Alf. Alf said ya was.

SANDY His folks are loaded.

ALAN I know!

SANDY Did – did Joe ever say anything?

ALAN Joe? What about?

SANDY About me gettin ugly, *arswipe.*

ALAN No, no Joe never said nothin.

SANDY Are ya sure?

ALAN Yeah. Yeah he never – he never said nothin! No! Why?

SANDY None of your business.

ALAN What's buggin you you got your pains?

SANDY No, I don't got my *pains* but I'm gonna get em if youse – if youse – well – no offence or nothin but when are youse gettin outa here anyways?

ALAN Soon as I get up the money I – wh – why is – is it buggin you me and Trese sleepin over?

SANDY Yeah. Yeah, it is it's – it's me and Joe gotta have – have some privacy, ya know? Ya know?

ALAN Yeah. Yeah I do I – I'll be out soon what can I say, we'll be out as soon as I got the cash.

SANDY I never heard of screwin your girlfriend on your buddy's floor.

ALAN I'll be out as soon as I got the cash, okay?

SANDY It's just strange you goin with Trese on our floor.

ALAN I know it's strange I know I'm strange I'm strange okay?

SANDY I know you're fuckin strange all right.

ALAN You're smokin too much. You're smokin too much.

SANDY Look who's talkin.

ALAN Well at least I know I'm doin it you don't even know. [*takes drag off cigarette*]

SANDY You're fuckin nuts, you know that, nuts.

ALAN I may be nuts but I fuckin know what I'm doin. I know I'm killin myself smokin these I know it so I'm throwin them away okay? I'm throwin them away! [ALAN *rips up his cigarettes and takes* SANDY's *cigarette out of her mouth*] Fuckin killsticks!

SANDY [*tries to stop him*] Stop it you – fuckin don't you touch me – you fucker you give me back the cash for those right now right now hear?

ALAN No! No Sandy I can't I don't have the money I gotta save it so I can fuck off outa this *hole* I don't have *money* okay??

SANDY [*starts to back out the door shaking head*] You're nuts Al –

ALAN [*grabs her back into the room*] I am not nuts. I am not nuts you understand? I just decided now I'm gonna quit smoking that's all. I got a flash in my head of my old man tryin to take his breath tryin to find the fuckin air and not gettin it fuckin all hunched over so's he wouldn't drown to death his his his feet all puffed all that shit all that shit comin out of his mouth and they wouldn't even clean it cause they said he couldn't get nothin cause he was gonna die so he had all this shit comin out of his mouth and and I know he didn't like it cause he was clean – all the *time* he was washin – and then when he's dyin they don't give a shit about his goddamn mouth with all the fuck comin out of it and they got a goddamn vacuum cleaner goin – we can't hear nothin and he keeps sort of movin forward movin ahead in his chair like when you're tryin not to crash out at the show so ya keep movin forward? He didn't want to go he didn't want to go at all and he went cause of these. Cause of these goddamn ugly white killsticks these! [*shows her cigarette, lets her go*] See? See why ya can't smoke? See?

SANDY [*very moved by Alan's speech; speaks quietly*] I don't know who the fuck you think you are tearin up the place just cause you seen your old man fuckin croak.

ALAN   You don't know what it's like, man, you don't know what it's like till you been there don't you talk.

SANDY   Don't tell me what I know, arswipe, don't you tell me nothin. I seen my mum go, I sat by her bed for three fuckin months and I don't go carryin on like a three-year-old.

ALAN   It wasn't the same I'm tellin ya it couldna been the same.

SANDY   And I'm a woman and I don't go cryin about it I never cried about it once.

ALAN   I'm not cryin about it I never cried about it I'm just tellin ya why not to smoke.

SANDY   You're just tellin me shit. Jeez if Joe seen you just now he'd think you were some kind of fag.

ALAN   I'm not a fag that's one thing I'm not I'm not a fag.

SANDY   Then start acting like a fuckin man.

ALAN   I'm not a fag you take that back.

SANDY   I'm not takin nothin back for no baby.

ALAN   I said take that back you ugly bitch.
         [*He grabs her. She throws him to the floor*]

SANDY   You're sad, you know that? You don't scare nobody.

ALAN   I'm no fag.

SANDY   [*goes back to lie on couch*] I seen ten-year-olds fight better than you.

ALAN   Why?

SANDY   Why what?

ALAN   Why don't I scare nobody?

SANDY   Cause you're a wimp that's why. Like one of them dogs that starts shakin when ya go to pat it.

ALAN   How come.

SANDY   How am I supposed to know?

ALAN   Don't say nothin to Joe, eh?

SANDY   What, about takin a fit?

ALAN   About you thinkin I'm like one of them dogs.

SANDY   I won't.

ALAN   Or Trese.

SANDY   Don't worry about it.

ALAN   You watched your mum go?

SANDY   Big deal.

ALAN   Couldna been the same.

SANDY It's all the same.

ALAN Don't you feel nothin?

SANDY Well I'm not a baby like you.

ALAN No.

SANDY Anyways bein dead ain't no different from livin anyway.

ALAN How do you know?

SANDY I just know. It's just like movin to Brockville or Oshawa or somethin. It ain't that different.

ALAN Oh no. Oh no you're wrong I think you're wrong there.

SANDY No I'm not.

ALAN Yes you are.

SANDY You don't know shit Al.

ALAN I do I do know some things and I know that. I know it's different.

SANDY Get out of my house.

ALAN I'm goin I didn't want to stay anyways it *smells* funny in here.

SANDY Garbage stinks up a place.

ALAN And Sandy.

SANDY *What.*

ALAN No offence or nothin, but you – you – are – you are gettin ugly lookin.
[SANDY *looks at him*]
See ya.

Act One, Scene Eight

JOE, SANDY, ALAN, THERESA *sitting in bar. Otis Redding's 'I've Been Loving You Too Long' is playing.*

JOE That's a shit hot tune. Too bad he died.

ALAN Did he die?

JOE That's right. In a fuckin motel.

ALAN That's too bad.

JOE Too bad Jimi Hendrix died too.

ALAN Yeah. Oh *yeah.* [*sings, drums*] 'Scuse me while I kiss the sky.'

JOE Did youse know if Hendrix hadda lived he was gonna join up with E.L.P.?

SANDY I seen them, Emerson, Lake and Palmer, down in Montreal.

JOE Ya know what they woulda been called if Hendrix hadda joined up with them?

ALAN Hendrix, and ...

JOE [*spells it out*] H.E.L.P. Help. And you fuckin would need help hearin those two play together.

ALAN Fuck would ya ever.

JOE Fuckin straight.

ALAN Would ya ever. Fuck, your brain'd die.

JOE H.E.L.P. *Help.*

THERESA I wouldn't need no help.

SANDY You don't got no ear for music.

THERESA I do so.

ALAN She sings and that all the time.

THERESA I seen Jerry uptown he got a job workin for Wilmot's.

SANDY That right eh.

JOE Splinter what a cocksuck.
     [*Restless,* JOE *goes to the jukebox, presses button.* JOE *walks to the urinal. After a moment,* ALAN *follows*]

THERESA He be workin with all that ice cream all the time. [*Pause*]

SANDY He could hardly munch out.

THERESA I love ice cream.

SANDY Just munch right out.

Act One, Scene Nine

JOE *and* ALAN. *In urinal of bar.*

ALAN Those two guys together. *Jeez!* [*shaking head in disbelief*]

JOE I'm goin buddy I'm takin off.

ALAN Where ya goin?

JOE That's for me to know.

ALAN Oh. Sorry. How – how come gettin sick of Kingston?

JOE Got me a job drivin a cat.

ALAN Jeez. You make a lot of cash doin that.

JOE Nice work if you can get it.

ALAN Nice work if you can get it.

JOE Make a shitload of money.

ALAN That's hard to do, drivin one of them things, ain't it?

JOE They're mother fuckers.

ALAN Jeez fuck where'd ya learn how to do that anyways?

JOE Hymie Beach.

ALAN Wow, I never knew that. You live down there?

JOE Sure, shared a motel room with this creep who later turned out to be a queer boy. Started sayin stuff about my dink and that when I got out of the shower. 'Is it always that long?'

ALAN Fuckin queers.

JOE I know.

ALAN They just make me – feel like pukin –

JOE I sent that one through the fuckin wall.

ALAN Did ya?

JOE Fuckin right.

ALAN I hate em.

[*Pause*]

JOE Don't say nothin to Sandy.

ALAN Don't she know?

[JOE *shakes his head*]

What if something happens – she gets cancer or somethin?

JOE What?

ALAN Them things happen, I've heard of them.

JOE ... I'll let ya know where I am.

ALAN Hey – I'd like to do that kind of shit.

JOE You should come out. You could get on a site dry-wallin or somethin.

ALAN They just take anybody?

JOE Sure.

ALAN No, no way.

JOE Suit yourself.

ALAN Hey – I forgot to tell ya, Cathy Yachuk jumped offa the Brock Towers!

JOE What?

ALAN Jumped right onto her feet Martin was sayin, fucked
em up so bad they hadda take a piece of her bum and
glue it on to her f-f-feet – so's she could walk on them.

JOE How come she done that?

ALAN She seen a white light in front of her, tellin her!

JOE Fuckin whore ... yuh, I'm gettin right out of this hole.

ALAN You comin back ever?

JOE How'm I sposda know?

Act One, Scene Ten

ALAN *on way to work, stumbles out door. There is an
Indian* MAN *on the street, his wrists bleeding heavily. He is
ambling past* ALAN. *He is very drunk.*

ALAN Hey buddy – hey can I do something for ya?

MAN [*drunk, mumbling*] Please ...

ALAN Hey, want a smoke?

MAN Yeah. Give me a smoke.

ALAN What are ya lookin for man?

MAN Fuckers took it fuckers.

ALAN Who? Did somebody jump ya? Eh? Did somebody
jump ya?

MAN Yaah. Some guys. Buncha Indians – fuckin Indians.

ALAN Hey man you're an Indian aren't ya?

MAN [*giggling*] Don't burn the fish bones! Don't burn the
fish bones!

ALAN That's okay man my fiancée she's Indian. Therese. I
like Indians it's okay.

MAN [*weeping like a girl*] Stupid fuckin Indians.

ALAN Hey. Hey don't cry. Is it hurtin bad? Please – just stay
here – I'll call an ambulance. Stay. [*starts to walk to
phone, holds up hand*] Stay.

MAN [*sits up, screams 'death scream'*] Aaaahh!
[ALAN *comes back, takes off his own shirt, ties it around
the* MAN's *wrist to stop the bleeding. The* MAN *sees a
vision*]
Devil-baby-eyes-devil-baby-eyes. Please. Please.
Mercy. Mercy. Hand. Gimme your hand. Hand.
Please.

ALAN What? You want me to hold your hand? Okay.
    [MAN *takes* ALAN's *hand, starts rubbing it in a sexual
    way.* ALAN *doesn't know what to do*]
MAN [*urgently*] Hey. Hey. Hey.
ALAN What, what is it, buddy?
MAN Hey. [*makes intercourse motion with fingers*] Let's tear
    off a piece. Come on let's tear off a piece. Rip off a
    piece. Come on.
ALAN Stupid cocksucker!
    [ALAN *flings* MAN *away, but* MAN *clings to his leg*]
    Get off me you fucker! Get offffffff me!
    [*he runs*]
MAN [*lies on street, giggling*] Pleeeeease. [*giggles*]
    [ALAN *jumps back to* SANDY's *living room where*
    THERESA *is asleep at his feet*]
ALAN [*yells*] Dieeeeeeeeeeee!

Act One, Scene Eleven

It is the middle of the night.
ALAN Therese?
THERESA Yeah?
ALAN Do you ever start thinkin ugly thoughts before ya go
    to sleep?
THERESA No, do you?
ALAN Yeah.
THERESA Like what?
ALAN Like fallin down and your teeth hittin the sidewalk.
THERESA Ewwwww.
ALAN Sometimes I even think of someone takin out my
    spine, like they do with a shrimp.
THERESA You crazy stupid-face, go sleepin and think of nice
    stuff.
ALAN Like what.
THERESA Doughnuts and the Wolfe Island ferry and that. Stuff
    like that.
ALAN Huh. I love ya Trese.
THERESA Madonna.

Act Two, Scene One

ALAN   Did you ever start thinkin somethin, and it's like ugly
...? And ya can't beat it out of your head? I wouldn't
be scared of it if it was sittin in front of me, I'd beat it
to shit – nothin wouldn't stop me – but I can't beat it
cause it's in my head fuck. It's not like bein crazy, it's
just like thinkin one thing over and over and it kinda
makes ya sick. Like when I was a kid and I used to
have these earaches all the time, you know? And I
would keep thinkin it was like a couple of garter
snakes with big ugly teeth all yellow, like an *old* guy's
teeth and there they were the two of them suckin and
bitin on my eardrum with these yellow teeth. Makin
noises like a cat eatin cat food. I could even hear the
fuckin noises. [*makes the noise*] Like that. Just made me
wanta puke thinkin that – made the pain worse I'd
think of their eyes, too, that made me sick, black eyes
lookin sideways all the time while they keep suckin
and chewin on my eardrum. Fuck. Do youse know
what I mean? No offense or nothin I don't mean no
offense I wish youse all good luck in your lives I was
just – like I just wanted to know if any of youse like
knew of a medicine or somethin ya might take for this
– they gotta have somethin cause the one I'm thinkin
of now is even worse it's fuckin bad it's it's somethin
Bonnie Cain told me about this nurse she knows goin
out to Enterprise out to one of the farms out there
these folks were on the dole so she goes up to see if the
kids got colds and that, and the wife, all small with
her teeth all black takes her into the warsh room and
tells her she got somethin wrong down in her
woman's part. And Bonnie said this nurse lifted up
this woman's skirt and you know what she seen? Like
a cauliflower growin out of her thing! A cauliflower!
Fuck! And ya know the worst part of it? When ya cut
it it bleeds! It grows blood and that! It just happened

last summer too, last fuckin summer in July! ... How'd
she go – like how'd she pee? Fuck I'll be doin the
dishes where I'm workin down the Tropicana there
and it's like pictures burning holes in my brain I try all
the time to like put other pictures over top of that, nice
things that I really get off on, eh, that I really like like –
like lambs in a field, you know, with the black on their
faces? Like baby sheep? I always liked them whenever
I seen one in a field or someplace I always laughed at
them so stupid lookin and cute fuck – I never told the
other guys they were there case they burn them or
something. Anyways I try puttin pictures of these
baby sheep over top of the cauliflower and I'll do it
and it's okay for a second then the lamb its eyes'll go
all funny like slits lookin sideways just like them
snakes and then it'll open its mouth and there'll be
them long sharp teeth and a bunch of worms inside
and the nice little sheep goes all ugly on me and the
cauliflower comes back worse than ever like it ate the
sheep or somethin.... Maybe if I could just have a car
or get back to workin on cars, you know? Or get into
Dragmasters, then maybe I'd stop thinkin of these
things. I don't know. I'm lookin for somebody who
knows, that's why I'm askin youse I don't know. I
wish I did. [*pause*] If it was in front of me I'd beat it to
shit, you know?

Act Two, Scene Two

ALAN *and* THERESA *at home.* ALAN *comes in after work.*
THERESA *is watching television, laughing.*

ALAN Did ya do it did ya get it done?

THERESA You got somethin on your mouth Al.

ALAN [*wipes*] What was it?

THERESA Look like cream from one of them Joe Louis.

ALAN What I got on my face don't matter, Trese, I asked ya a
question.

THERESA What?

ALAN Did ya get what I told ya done?

THERESA Readin writin?

ALAN Yes.

THERESA Shhhh baby sleepin Al.

ALAN Did – let's see. Awwwww hey Danny! He's not sleepin! Hey ya little bugger how ya doin – this is your dad – this is your dad speakin, ya know me? Hey? He does, he knows me. Don't ya Danny. Hey Danny did your angel mummy do what daddy asked her to? Eh? Yes? She did? Oh thank you Danny you are the most neatest cutest little baby boy – what's that on his chin?

THERESA From eatin milk.

ALAN Theresa you don't *eat* milk you drink it.

THERESA I know.

ALAN There. Wipe that ugly milk offa ya. Eh Danny? You are my little bugger and I'm your daddy! Hey! Your mummy gonna show me what she done! Okay mummy, now show me what ya done.

THERESA I lost it.

ALAN How could you lose it?

THERESA I done it, Al, but I lost it.

ALAN *Theresa.* Theresa I'm gonna try not to get mad at ya but ya can't keep doin this to me! Every day you're tellin me ya lost your homework!

THERESA Maybe someone take it.

ALAN Theresa don't you understand I am tryin to improve my family.

THERESA [*coyly*] Al.

ALAN What.

THERESA [*delighted*] You shoulda seen the pooh I done today it was hardly long!

ALAN Theresa married ladies with babies ain't supposed to say things like that!

THERESA Sorry.

ALAN Danny could hear ya ya know.

THERESA I don't think he hear Al I think he deaf.

ALAN What?

THERESA I shoutin in his ear he don't do nothin.
ALAN Trese ya don't go shoutin in babies' ears!
[*She kisses him. He melts*]
THERESA I love ya Al.
ALAN You know I love you don't ya you know it – more than anything in this whole world you and Danny boy.
THERESA I know Al. How many dishes you done today?
ALAN Two hundred and twenty-three.
THERESA Jeez.
ALAN Yup. That's ten more than yesterday.
THERESA Jeez.

Act Two, Scene Three

THERESA *has been sleeping over at* SANDY's *because* SANDY *is scared. Cat scream.*
SANDY What's that noise. Trese wake up. Hear that?
THERESA What?
SANDY Listen – oh Jesus what is it?
THERESA Maybe it Charlie Manson.
SANDY Oh shut up you watch too much TV.
THERESA Maybe it a pussy cat.
SANDY Hello? Hello? Anybody there? Trese hand me somethin. The lamp.
THERESA Why?
SANDY Shut your mouth and don't ask questions.
THERESA Okay okay here.
SANDY Okay. You get the knife from the top drawer just in case he comes in here.
THERESA Who Charlie Manson.
SANDY Don't say that name Trese. Scream if anybody comes....
THERESA I will Sandy.
[SANDY *goes to other room. She screams a primal scream*]
SANDY [*returns*] It was nothin.
THERESA How come.
SANDY Cause.

THERESA How come my baby never smilin?

SANDY Are ya doin what the workers tell ya?

THERESA Al do it he don't let me do nothin.

SANDY Why?

THERESA He smarter.

SANDY I guess so.

THERESA He love Danny. He wash him with soap and he feed
him and he huggin him.

SANDY What's he feedin him.

THERESA Bologna.

SANDY At four months?

THERESA He love it.

SANDY Oh Christ. Don't ya have baby food.

THERESA I don't know.

SANDY What am I gonna do with you?

THERESA I'm glad I stayin here. Al cryin nights.

SANDY How come?

THERESA I don't know. I tell him nothin's wrong everything fine
but he keep cryin.

SANDY Trese do ya think Joe'll come back?

THERESA He proly comin back next Friday.

SANDY If he do, he can go to hell.

THERESA Bonnie Cain say he never comin back.

SANDY She did?

THERESA She don't know nothin. He comin back.

SANDY I got a letter.

THERESA Ya did?

SANDY I burnt it though, didn't read it.

THERESA Sandy you depress?

SANDY No. I just don't like stayin alone nights it ain't good for
ya.

THERESA You could come stayin with us.

SANDY Uh uh. No way. I don't want to see no baby eatin
bologna.

THERESA Oh.

SANDY You get in some baby food, Trese, or I'm reporting ya
to the social worker.

THERESA Okay.

SANDY Okay?

THERESA I'm gonna.

SANDY   You go on to sleep. Now.
THERESA   Night Sandy. Don't go havin no bad dreams.
SANDY   Night.
[THERESA *falls asleep instantly.* SANDY *stays awake, staring out.*]

Act Two, Scene Four

ALAN *has just been fired from his dishwashing job. He is thrown out of a door, real or imaginary, onto a busy street. He has stolen an egg, which he carries in his hand.*
ALAN   [*holding up egg as pointer*] I was quittin anyways, ya bastards, there's white worms in the hamburg, I *seen* em, there's white worms in the hamburg! [*more quietly, to himself*] I seen em wiggle – [*turning to audience, in threatening tones*] There wasn't no egg on that pan, sir, there wasn't no egg on that frypan.
[ALAN *stares at the audience for a moment, gets the idea to throw the egg at the door and turns very slowly towards door. Then in a flash, starts to throw the egg but instead, cracks it over his head. He puts the shell in his pocket, sees somebody in the distance, slicks down his hair, leans onto the sewer and discovers the Indian* MAN *with a bottle.* ALAN *grabs it and takes a sip*]
MAN   Man who is standing between two girly-girls in the whirly-burl.
ALAN   Oh why don't ya just shut up....
MAN   [*pointing at constellation in the sky*] Double devil – stuck together – cha cha cha!
[JOE *appears, wearing a new coat and a hat that says 'success.'* ALAN *rushes to greet him. By the end of the scene, they reach the entrance to* SANDY's *apartment*]
ALAN   Jesus Joe! Joe! Hey Joe, how're ya doin?
JOE   Hey buddy how are you?
ALAN   Okay, you know, hangin on. You – when did ya get back?
JOE   Just now, buddy, but not for long. I'm moving Sandy out there with me.

ALAN No kidding? It's pretty good out there?

JOE It's a great place, man, lots of work, nice people. Hell of a lot better than this hole, I'm tellin you.

ALAN Yeah? Does Sandy know you're back?

JOE Nope. I'm gonna surprise her. She'll be happy as hell to see me. Then the two of us are gonna take right off.

ALAN That right? ... Hey me and Theresa got a kid – a little boy, Danny.

JOE Is that right? Danny, huh? So how do you like bein a father?

ALAN It's all right, man. I like it. I make a good father I guess.

JOE Yeah? ... Well, I better head off.

ALAN Hey – Joe – I got somethin to tell ya.

JOE Is this a long story or a short one?

ALAN Not too long – d'ju hear about Boyd's GTO?

JOE What the one that used to be parked on Johnson below Division?

ALAN Yeah, you know, green with chrome mags and chrome cut outs.

JOE Yeah. What a fuckin beast. What about it?

ALAN He totalled it.

JOE Hah. Well it was a shitty lookin car anyways.

ALAN Yeah but fuck it had – it had them high lift cam solid lifters, and, and high compression kit and –

JOE You name it.

ALAN He had it. Yup. Hey – did you know it had four fuckin carbs?

JOE Eat shit.

ALAN No kiddin, four! But you know how come he kept it lookin so shitty?

JOE Beats me.

ALAN So the cops wouldn't notice. They all knew, though eh, they knew what he had. Fuck that thing was fast he used to shoot the main drag doin one-fifty.

JOE Yeah? That's fast.

ALAN Fuckin fast. You know how he totalled it?

JOE No.

ALAN Fuck it was funny. We were gettin polluted up at the Manor, eh, and Alfie decides he's gonna go up to Gan. He was about half pissed I guess. So parently he tries to pass three or four cars same time except one of em happens to be a truck goin left. So I guess he almost makes it but the truck catches him by his back right fender and spins him. Huh. Flipped the car six fuckin times.

JOE Jeez. How is he?

ALAN Alfie? He's okay now but he got stabbed in the heart with the rearview mirror. Had an operation.

JOE That right?

ALAN Chuck was with him and –

JOE The Scotty?

ALAN Yeah and he just jumped out and never even had a scratch on him. What's that a present for the wife?

JOE Yeah. That Charlie perfume shit.

ALAN Hardly nice. Yeah, that's nice stuff. Women – they like that kinda stuff.

JOE I know. Smells shitty to me.

ALAN Yeah.

JOE Well I gotta move buddy catch you later.

ALAN Hey! Hey! [*From his pocket,* ALAN *takes an ornamental iron monk with a hard on. It is wrapped in newspaper*] Here.

JOE What's this?

ALAN Just somethin.

JOE Oh yeah. I seen one of these. Well I'm gone.

ALAN See ya.... Bye Joe!

Act Two, Scene Five

SANDY *and* JOE *seated at a table.*

SANDY I got a fucking hole in my gut cause of you.

JOE Who told ya that.

SANDY Doctor Scott.

JOE He don't know what he's talking about.

SANDY Hurtin me all the time I had pain.

JOE Not no more. Not no more ya won't.

SANDY I was takin pills even – prescription!

JOE I told ya babe I feel bad.

SANDY I never done nothin to you *why*??

JOE Ewwww Christ I missed your body there was times I wanted ya so bad I could taste ya. I'd lie in bed there and think about you and what ya looked like stripped naked, think about your nice titties.

SANDY Two old bags.

JOE *Nothin* them are peaches.

SANDY Bullshit. I'm not goin back with ya.

JOE Yes you are.

SANDY Can't push me around no more.

JOE Come on just try it a couple weeks if ya don't like it you can fuck off.

SANDY Won't be nothin different.

JOE It's gotta be different.

SANDY It'll be the same as before, beatin up on me.

JOE No way.

SANDY How the fuck do I know?

JOE Cause it's fuckin true that's how.

SANDY I hate you. I hated you all the time you was gone.

JOE I know.

SANDY I woulda laughed if you hadda died.

JOE I never did.

SANDY I know.

JOE So.

[*Pause*]

SANDY How come ya want me back.

JOE Don't know. It's dog shit when you're gone.

SANDY Then why'd ya stay so long.

JOE Shit Sandy.

SANDY I was up nights shakin.

JOE Scared of the crackwalker were ya?

SANDY He never hurt nobody.

JOE I missed makin it with ya. Did ya miss it with me?

SANDY I didn't have no one.

JOE That's cause you're mine.

SANDY Is that right.

JOE [*opens her gift*] Here. Smell that.

SANDY Hmmn.

JOE You told me you like that shit.

SANDY It's okay.

JOE Soooo. You been workin for Nikos?

SANDY Some.

JOE What else you been doin?

SANDY Learned how to make a new drink.

JOE What, rum and Coke?

SANDY That's not new.

JOE What, dough brain.

SANDY A Dirty Mother, asshole.

JOE A dirty mother asshole, what's that?

SANDY A Dirty Mother! It's tequila, crème de cacao, and milk. It's hardly good.

JOE Sounds like a chocky milkshake from Mexico.

SANDY Arswipe. I got a batch made up in the fridge, you want one?

JOE Yeah, okay. I'll try one. Gimme a beer with it though.

SANDY [she goes to the kitchen; from kitchen] You should give Al a call he's in a bad way.

JOE Yeah I seen him he looked like shit.

SANDY They got a kid, Danny.

JOE He was tellin me.

SANDY It's a medical retard.

JOE Fuuuuck.

SANDY It don't ever move its face – like a doll.

JOE See this thing he give me?

SANDY What is it?

JOE I don't know. An iron monk with a hard on?

SANDY Jeez where'd he get that up at Van's?

JOE I guess so.

[SANDY brings in tray]

Well fuckin jumpqueen, eh, where'd ya get them glasses?

SANDY My girlfriend Gail she scoffed em offa the 401 Inn.

JOE Fuckin eh.

SANDY They'd cost ya, ya know.

JOE Hmmm. That's ahhh that's a shit hot drink.

SANDY Me and Gail drink it all the time when we go out.

JOE It's not bad.

SANDY We always order it only none of em knows how to make it so we have to tell them.

JOE Yeah?

SANDY I can make any kind of drink now she taught me.

JOE What're you doin two women goin drinkin alone together.

SANDY Who said we were alone?

JOE Come here.

SANDY Joe it ain't like that no more.

JOE Who said it ain't.

SANDY I did. Keep your paws offa me.

JOE Jeez you're lookin good.

SANDY I'm doin my eyeliner different.

JOE Yeah?

SANDY Makes my eyes look bigger.

JOE Nice.

SANDY I know.

Act Two, Scene Six

ALAN *and* THERESA's *place.* THERESA *is playing with the baby. There are tea things set out. The baby does not respond to anything.*

THERESA Beebeebeebee ... How come you not drinkin your tea, beebee? You got a bad cold? Poor beebee. [*singing*] My little baby is my baby my little Danny is my angel baby I take care of him, and he don't cry or nothin and he ain't never gonna have the crib death neither – [*speaking*] No way Danny, cause I love ya. Al loves ya too but he a bastard sometime I know he don't talk nice in front of you sometime – don't you go goin into one of them deep sleeps beebee – no – hey! Hey baby Danny! Wake up cause that's how them other babies got the crib death! From sleepin too deep! S'true! You darlin little baby! You mine! That sosha worker's hardly nice, eh? Look! [*dangles Joe Louis wrapper in front of Danny*] Look at that baby, you like that? Eh? It's hardly pretty! You come on, come on, gimme a smile beebee; you thinkin too much just like Al that why you so serious all the time. Ohhhhhbaby [*she rocks him*] so soff. Skin hardly soff. Hey! I look like that madonna lady and she holdin baby Jesus just like I holdin you so you mus look like Jesus! Baby Jesus! Oooohhh Danny you my beebee Jesus and I the Madonna lady and Al maybe he Joseph, he make stuff outa wood. You like a little horsey made outa wood carry you down Princess Street when we go to the S & R? I love ya beebee. That a little smile? Oh! Oh baby baby Jesus I love Ya!

ALAN [*comes blasting through the door, starts tearing up the place – medicines, creams, clothes, everything*] No fuckin social worker's gonna fuckin tell me how to run my fuckin life! I don't take this fuckin shit from nobody! Nobody don't tell me what to do and nobody don't tell me how to take care of my baby never! That means you too you fuckin woman – I'm not takin any shit from you neither! There. We're not using any of their cocksucking medicine – they'll try to kill you with it!

THERESA Al! Al stop it!

ALAN They did they killed my dad with all their fuckin medicine! He didn't have no hair and he didn't have no flesh just bones all over and ugly and yellow. No way Therese no way you could stop me I'm throwin it all fuckin out! Out the window, watch! There! It's out the window! Danny! Hey Danny my boy my own son see? You don't have to be takin any of that ugly tastin shit no more!

THERESA But he gonna get numona if he don't take his medicine doctor say so! Nurse say he hafta take it three time a day or he gettin worse! Doctor sees you done that he won't give us no more medicine for Danny! You basard! You basard! [*she hits him*]

ALAN Arswipe! Don't you know nothin? Don't you know them doctors make money offa sick babies? That's why they like to keep em sick with all them medicines! So they make more fuckin money!

THERESA I don't believe ya. Doctors are nice they wouldn't go makin babies sick!

ALAN Jeez you're a dumbrain sometimes, Therese, they don't give a fuck about our fuckin baby so long as they

get their TVs and golf clubs and that. They care dick!
That's why they give em this poison so the baby stay
sick!

THERESA It not poison, it good for ya, the nurse say so! She
don't even have no TV, she tole me. So you're crazy I
know that stuff good for Danny he gettin better
already!

ALAN That baby ain't gettin no better you stupid woman
you know it ain't. It looks strange. It don't look right
and that's cause they're givin it all them fuckin
medicines! Fuck them! So no more!

THERESA Really would them doctors do that? Really?

ALAN Fuckin right they would. Bastards.

THERESA Bastards. How come? How come they hurtin my little
baby?

ALAN Money. Money and bucks. Cocksuckers.

THERESA Well what we gonna do about all his snifflin and that?

ALAN Well I know what to do the social worker even said I
did. He said I was a great father and you even heard
him. I was a great father.

THERESA S'true Alan.

ALAN Well, it got a cold, right? So if ya got a cold, ya gotta
get warm, what else? It's fuckin simple and them
doctors always do everything to make it harder! Fuck!
So all we do, is ahh – turn on the oven! It's easy! Here.
Put it to about five hundred – there – and open the
door like that – and – now bring him over –

THERESA Why? What you gonna do?

ALAN Just bring the baby over, Trese. Do what I tell ya!

THERESA Al you not cooking the baby, are ya? [*weeping with
confusion*]

ALAN [*laughs*] Huh. Wait'll I tell Joe that he'll laugh. Cookin
the baby. Right. Jesus arshole it's just like at the farm
back in Picton when mum used to sit by the stove with
Ronny to warm him up that's all! It's easy! If a guy's
got a cold, warm him up!

THERESA Oh. Don't make it too hot though.

ALAN Keep out of it, woman. [*places crib as close to stove as he
can get it*] There. There ya go Danny! How you doin
anyway you little bugger – that's right it's your daddy

he come to make you better! Getcha away from all them fuckin doctors! That's right.

THERESA Al he's coughin! Can't we get back some of that cough syrup?

ALAN Listen stupid we're not usin any of that stuff I told ya! Didn't ya hear me or what? Listen. If he's coughin we'll just get that Vicks vapour rub that my old man used to use.

THERESA That stuff smell too much!

ALAN If it's good enough for my old man it's good enough for my baby Therese. He used to put it all over his chest and his cough be gone the nex day. Here. [*he puts a whole jar of Vicks over the baby's body*]

THERESA Al you puttin too much!

ALAN Don't tell me what to do! Shut up! I know what I'm doin I told ya the social worker said I was a great father! So shut up! [*he holds the baby up. It is glistening with the stuff*] There. You're gonna be just fine now baby.

THERESA Al you sure it ain't too much.

ALAN Shhhhh. He's goin to sleep. Come here. I got somethin for ya.

THERESA You did? What'dja get donuts?

ALAN [*opens perfume – orange, cheap, and it has broken in the package*] Shit. It broke on me. It's okay though here I'll put it in a glass. [*he does so*] There. [*hands it to her*]

THERESA Smell that. That's hardly beautiful Al. Thank you I love perfume.

ALAN I know ya do. Ya like it?

THERESA I love it. It hardly smells nice.

ALAN [*caresses her*] Guess why I brung it?

THERESA Why?

ALAN I love you and you're my angel madonna.

THERESA A-l-l-l-l-l.

ALAN It's true. Come here angel. Hey. Ehhey. You know I love makin love to ya. I love fuckin you and chewin ya out. [*whispers*] I do.

THERESA I know.

[ALAN *starts to undress her. They start necking on the floor next to the baby.* THERESA *stops suddenly*]

THERESA Oh oh.

ALAN What?

THERESA We can't do it Al.

ALAN Don't matter if you're bleedin.

THERESA No I can't do it till I get my new IUD in. Or I get pregnant again doctor say so!

ALAN Fuck the goddamn doctors! Goddamn doctors trying to run my life saying I can't make love to my own woman to my own wife fuck em fuck em. I don't care if you get pregnant we're gonna do it when we want and no doctor's gonna tell us nothin.

THERESA No! No Alan, please! Get off me you bastard we're not doin it today no way! No! Get offa me or I callin the cops.

ALAN [*he hits her, sends her across the room*] You stupid dumb cunt Indian bitch face fat fat retarded whore. I don't want ya anyways! [*he collapses on floor, now meeker, almost whiny*] Alls I wanted was a little lovin anyways there's nothin wrong with that? A man is sposda get lovin from his woman ain't he? That is how come ya get married, ain't it? All I wanted was a little lovin that's all ... that's alllll.

[*The baby is crying*]

Look what you done woman you makin the baby cry! You stupid bitch!

[THERESA *gets up to go to the baby*]

No! No you stay down I'm the only one who can make him stop cryin. Watch. Hey baby. Hey baby here's your daddy. He's a great daddy, huh? Eh?

[*The baby is screaming*]

THERESA Take it away from the stove Alan! Take it away from the stove!

ALAN [*to* THERESA] Shhhhh. [*to baby*] Come on baby stop that cryin daddy don't like it when you cryin! Shhhh. Now shhhhhh. Gonna buy you a car when you get older – what kind you want, a Monte Carlo? Okay. I'm gonna get you a Monte Carlo. You wait, I'm gonna get work in a station and I'm gonna buy my own and I'm gonna get you anything you want. Okay? Now shhhhhhhh. Stop cryin I'm gonna get you a Monte

Carlo didn't ya hear me? Didn't ya? Shhhhhh. Be
quiet your mum is tryin to sleep, okay? Shhhhhh!
Come on, come on. My little Danny boy baby. Come
onnnn. Shhhhhhhh! [*on the last 'shhh' he squeezes the
baby's neck till it dies*] Shhhhhh. [*from now on he is very
wooden, like a sleepwalker. Looks at* THERESA, *who is
watching in wonder*] It's okay. It's okay it's not cryin
any more. See. It's quiet now. It's not cryin. I – I – I
done it, see? See? I'm a good father he – you know
how come he stopped? Cause I told him he was gonna
get a Monte Carlo.

THERESA What's that?

ALAN It's a kind of car. It's a place too. One of them south
sea islands. Maybe we'll go there, eh? Anyways I gotta
go I gotta meet somebody ... see ya.
[ALAN *goes.* THERESA *looks after him.*]

Act Two, Scene Seven

JOE *and* SANDY's. ALAN, JOE *and* SANDY *are watching a
Leafs hockey game on television.* ALAN *is sitting away
from* JOE *and* SANDY, *and he is smoking and loudly eating
barbecue chips.* JOE *and* SANDY *are very much involved
with each other and the game, and they virtually ignore*
ALAN.

JOE Go go go you fucker – Bunnyfuck what are you fuckin
doin – *get him off Nykoluk get him off the ice fuck.*

ALAN Imlach dies.
[JOE *does not respond*]
IMLACH DIES!!

JOE Oh LAROUQUE – come on Sittler put that mother in
come on come on FUCK OFF PERRAULT, do it Daryl
hey Martin Martin put it in put it ALL RIGHT! [*jumps
up*] ALL FUCKING RIGHT!
[ALAN *jumps up with* JOE, *leans into the TV, his face only
one inch away from the screen, screams, wagging his head*]

ALAN ALLLLL FUCKIN RIIIIIIIGHT! [*looks back at* JOE *with
a little laugh*]

SANDY [*jocularly*] Take a bird why don't ya?

[ALAN *continues yelling into TV*]

JOE Hey Al don't scare the TV away he –

[THERESA *appears in the doorway with a bag in her hand.*
She is reminiscent of Cassandra in The Trojan Women]

THERESA YOU TOLE HIM YOU GIVE HIM A MONTE CARLO
AND YA DON'T EVEN DRIVE ONE. *YA DON'T*
EVEN DRIVE ONE.

[*Her presence is so strong that she immediately captures*
their attention]
I not goin screwin with ya no more Al, no way. No
way! You stoppem breathin. I tell him 'Breathin baby,
breathin' and he not cause *you stoppenim.*

ALAN [*looking away from* THERESA] She's lyin you guys, stop
your lyin.

THERESA You goin up the river to Penetang, Al, you goin there
tomorrow and you never comin out for what you
done you not goin back with me I goin with Ron
Harton he better than you he not stoppem breathin, he
still livin up on Division up at Shuter's? I callin him up
and I goin steady with him he better lookin you funny
lookin I screwin him.

ALAN You lyin fat cow you don't know what you're fuckin
talkin about crazy fucking whore-bag – LIAR!
[ALAN *knocks* THERESA *to the floor, hesitates, grabs two*
glasses half-full of Dirty Mother, and runs off. JOE *follows*]

THERESA You got a doughnut, Sanny, gimme a doughnut.

SANDY What have ya got in the bag, Trese.

THERESA Ivy, Ivy gimme the bag, I not givin it.

SANDY What's in it, though.

THERESA I takin him up the graveyard.

SANDY What for.

THERESA I puttin him with Grandma down St. Mary's Sanny,
see ya later.

SANDY [*stepping in front of* THERESA'*s exit*] Wait a minute
what –

THERESA Fuck off Sandy.

SANDY What's inside it.

[THERESA *giggles.* SANDY *touches the bag, flinches*]

SANDY I'm callin the cops.

THERESA Agghhhhh. You fuckin call anyone I takin one of my fits.

SANDY I'm shakin in my shoes, Trese. [*begins to dial*]

THERESA [*grabs* SANDY, *rips phone from wall*] You not callin –

SANDY [*gets up, begins to exit, turns around, points at* THERESA] You're not here when I get back and I'm tellin Ron Harton what ya done down the Lido, ya hear me? [THERESA *stares at* SANDY *in horror*] I will, too.

THERESA Okay.

SANDY I mean it. [*exits*]

THERESA [*to baby in bag*] It okay, Danny, don't you be cryin now, you with baby Jesus sittin on the cloud and the Virgin lookin like me she with ya she sittin there wearin that long blue dress goin down to her feet hardly pretty, eh? ... Danny? You still live? You breathin if I breathin into ya? S'okay I'm your mum! [*tries to breathe into baby*] Danny? You dead, eh? You not live. You never comin back, eh. [*puts bag to side, picks up severed phone, does not dial*] Hi Janus won't be doin readin writin today. Somethin happen. Just somethin. The baby die. The baby die. Up at Sanny's. Okay okay I waitin ... Ron Harton still livin up at Shuter's? [*hangs up the phone, and picks it up immediately*] C'I speak to Ron please? Hi Ron, it's Trese. S'okay if we start goin together I love ya. Okay, see ya Tuesday. [SANDY *enters, breathless, leans against the door. She cannot look at* THERESA]

SANDY Don't want you tellin no stories to the cops, you hear me? Want you to tell em the truth exactly like it happened, okay?

THERESA Don't like ya no more, Sanny.

SANDY S'too bad.

THERESA You a dirty faggot.

SANDY Right.

THERESA Not my friend no more!

SANDY Okay....

THERESA I not talkin to YOU. [*She turns her back to* SANDY. *She is crying.* SANDY *notices*]

SANDY   You should come out to Calgary sometime – visit.

THERESA No Sanny, I workin!

SANDY   What?

THERESA [*tells story joyously with no trace of grief*] Down at
Kresge's up with Ivy. Hah! She hardly funny she
hardly get pissed off when I eatin icin she yellin
'Trese, if you eat one more chocolate icin I tellin
Charlie,' so I go 'You tellin Charlie I tellin on you, Ivy,
snitchin butter tarts!' They're hardly good, though,
them tarts. Ivy English ... Sorry I can't comin with ya
out west, Sanny ... Ivy be piss off.

Act Two, Scene Eight

ALAN *and Indian* MAN *on warm air vent.* ALAN *is
leaning against wall. He is clanging two glasses together.
This produces a spooky sound.*

ALAN   [*pointing to* MAN] You fuckin touch me and I'll break
your head.

MAN   Hee hee hee Church 'n Mondee all dee Mondee hee
hee hee!

ALAN   I will break your fuckin head in!

MAN   [*starts happily, becomes angry as he remembers incident
with a paramedic who denied him phenobarbital*] Breakin
my fa fa pheno phenobarbidoll – barbidoll – NIGGER,
YOU NIGGER!

ALAN   Shut it you fuck, just shut it.

       [MAN *in panic, rushes toward the audience*]

MAN   SHUT THE WINDOW, SHUT THE WINDOW, SHUT
THE WINDOW.... [*laughs*]

ALAN   Nothing's funny, okay, so – just – STOP LAUGHIN.
Just pass out will ya, can't ya just pass out?
       [MAN *vomits on* ALAN's *sock*]
Ahhhh fuck you goddamn *shit*. SHIT! Eccchh you
keep your puke to yourself you old fuck!
       [*crouches, rocking*] I could drive a Monte Carlo I know I
could. [*rubbing glasses together*]

[JOE *enters, looking for* ALAN, *spots him, then crosses to him*]

JOE Al?

ALAN Joe!

JOE Look – ah –

ALAN She's lyin Joe, I could drive a Monte Carlo.

JOE Al?

ALAN I could *drive one easy.*

JOE You could drive any car on the road. Now why don't you come on –

ALAN I – I – I can't.

JOE Why not?

ALAN I – I – I'm too cold, you know? I'm freezin.

JOE You're okay, ya probably got a flu; ya got a bug, okay?

ALAN No, no, I don't got a bug, I'm just cold; he puked on me.

JOE So he puked on ya Martin used to puke on ya all the time. Come on – come on out of that shit pit and I'll get ya a coffee.

ALAN NO. No, I don't want to, I just don't want to, okay?

JOE Suit yourself. [*turns his back on* ALAN, *starts to leave*]

ALAN I done what I done and I done it and I fucked it up so I'm payin for it, get it? I'm payin for it.

JOE I don't know what ya done.

ALAN Sorry, Joe.

[JOE *looks at him, can't think of what to say*]

Joe.

JOE Yeah.

ALAN Could ya do one thing?

JOE What.

ALAN Tell her I could drive a Monte Carlo. Easy.

JOE I will.

ALAN Bye Joe. [*crouches in previous position, zipping and unzipping his jacket*] Nobody here – but us chickens – nobody here but us guys – don't bother me we got work to do and eggs to lay – and guys to see –

MAN SHHHHHHHHHHHHHhhhhhhhhhh. [*with no motion, just the sound*]

Act Two, Scene Nine

SANDY I think it's better off dead. I'm not kiddin ya I'm
serious. It don't hurt babies to be dead they go straight
on up to heaven no hell no purgatory no nothin *no
problems.* Cause their souls are still white as snow –
they ain't had the time to get them black and ugly. Not
like the rest of us – oh no if a baby dies he's just fine he
don't even know he's dead. Youse shoulda seen him
lyin there in that casket he looked fine. They had them
little pajamas on him Trese got up at the S and R, the
ones with all them dogs chasin cats all over, all
yellow? They hardly looked sweet. And they had a big
wreath of flowers around his neck so's to hide the
strangle – you know the kind you put on your door at
Christmas? Like that. It was kinda nice. We all lined
up to take a look at him too – first time he got so much
attention in his life – nobody broke up or nothin not
even Trese. In fact I was scared she was gonna break
up laughin. I'm not kiddin ya it don't bug her at all the
kid's gone. Jeez y'know I don't know what goes on
inside that girl but it ain't what's goin on inside the
rest of us. She only got one thing on her mind now
that's goin after Ron Harton. Don't ask me *why,* he
looks like the fucking wrath of God. He's a pig too. I
don't blame Trese though, I still feel for her even –
fuck – this old bag sittin behind me was goin on about
how come Trese never went to the hairdressers, you
know what her hair is like, eh, right in the middle of
the service, so I turn around and I says, 'You're gonna
hardly think of goin to the hairdressers when your
own baby's just been killed by your own husband, ya
fuckin old hag.' I called her that too, right to her face.
Oh yeah I'll stand up for a friend, anytime. I'll tell ya
who else I stood up for at that service ... Al, and he
done it. Oh yeah, I still consider him a friend. No
matter what he done, nobody can say what happened

70

in that room; so I walk into the funeral parlour, and I take one of them cookies they got lyin out, you know, just tea biscuits, and I turn around and who's standin behind me lookin me right in the eye but that goddamn Bonnie Cain. She comes up close her breath just reekin and she says to me how she seen the whole thing from the window and how he done it with a plastic bag one of them Glad Bags and how Trese was lookin on and laughin. That goddamn holy bitch. You lie I says to her and I grab her by the tit and I says 'You fuckin hound dog one more word outa you and I send you to your goddamn grave.' ... He never done it with a plastic bag he done it with his hands. I woulda I woulda broke every bone in her fuckin body and she knowed it too. *She* didn't say nothin more. Jeez I'll be glad to get outa this hole I'm tellin ya. I won't miss it neither I won't even dream about it. I won't. I worry about Trese but she'll be okay, you know? She'll – she'll go back down the Lido, start blowin off old queers again for five bucks. It's still open it won't never close. ... They had them flowers round Danny's neck so's to hide the strangle but I seen it. The flowers never hid it they just made ya look harder, ya know? They just made ya look harder.

Act Two, Scene Ten

Small struggle offstage. THERESA *runs onstage.*

THERESA Stupid old bassard don't go foolin with me you don't even know who I look like even. You don't even know who I lookin like.

Pink

Notes

This monologue was commissioned for the Arts Against Apartheid Benefit in Toronto in the spring of 1986. It was performed by Clare Coulter.

Pink

LUCY, *a ten-year-old white girl talking to her dead black nurse, Nellie, shot in a march, in her open coffin.*

LUCY NELLIE NELLIE NELLIE NELLIE NELLIE NELLIE NELLIE NELLIE NELLIE NELLIE NELLIE NELLIE NELLIE NELLIE NELLIE NELLIE

NELLIE NELLIE NELLIE NELLIE NELLIE NELLIE NELLIE I want you to come back, to shampoo my hair and make a pink cake and we can sit in the back and roll mealie pap in our hands see, I told you not to go in those marches and I told you, I told you that what you guys don't understand, what you didn't see, is apartheid's for YOU. IT'S FOR YOUR GUYS FEELINGS, see, like we got separate washrooms cause you like to spit, and if we said, 'Eww yucch, don't spit,' it would hurt your feelings and we got separate movies, cause you like to talk back to movie stars and say 'amen' and 'that's the way' and stuff and that drives us crazy so we might tell you to shut up and then you might cry and we got separate bus stops cause you don't like deodorant cause you say it smells worse than people and we might tell you you stink and the only thing I don't get is how come you get paid less for the same job my Mummy says it's because you people don't like money anyway, you don't like TVs and stereo's and all that stuff cause what you really like to do is sing and dance. And you don't need money to sing and dance I just ... I don't understand why you weren't happy with us, Mummy let you eat as much sugar as you wanted, and we never said anything to you, some days, Mummy says it was up to a quarter-pound, but we know blacks like sugar so we didn't mind, and we even let you take a silver spoon, I heard Mummy say to her friends, 'there goes another silver spoon to Soweto' but she never called the police ... and you had your own little room

back there, and we even let your husband come once
in a while, and that's against the law, Mummy and
Daddy could have gone to jail for that, so how come
you weren't grateful? How come you stopped singing
those Zulu songs in the morning, those pretty songs
like the one that was about love and kissing, you
stopped singing, and you stopped shampooing my
hair, you said I could do it myself, and and your eyes,
your eyes used to look at me when I was little they
would look at me like they were tickling me just
tickling me all the time, like I was special, but they
went out, they went out like a light does and you
stopped making my cakes every Tuesday, every
Tuesday morning I would ask you to make me a pink
cake and you would always say, 'you ask your
mummy' and then you'd make it, but you stopped
making them, you told me I was too old for pink
cakes, that the pink wasn't real, it was just food colour
anyway and then, and then, you hardly ever came
anymore, and when I saw you that day ... when I saw
you downtown with your husband and four children
all ... hanging off your arms, I just couldn't stand it! I
wanted to yell at your children and tell them you were
mine that you were more mine than theirs because
you were with me more much more so you were mine
and to let go of you to get off you and I hated the way
you looked without your uniform, so brown and
plain, not neat and nice anymore, you looked so pretty
in your uniform, so pretty, but we didn't even mind
when you didn't want to wear it.

We didn't mind, but you were still unhappy, and
when I saw you in town looking so dusty and you
didn't even introduce me to your kids and one of
them, one of them did that rude thing that
'Amandilia' thing that means black power I saw you
slap his hand but you didn't say anything, so you
must have hated me too, I saw that you hated me too
and I'd been so nice to you, I told you my nightmares
and you changed my bed when I wet it and now you
didn't even like me and it wasn't my fault it wasn't

my fault it just when I asked you why that day, you
were cleaning the stove and I said Nellie why ...
don't you like me anymore, and you said, 'you're not a child
anymore, Lucy, you're a white person now' and it
wasn't my fault I couldn't help it I couldn't help
yelling

SLAVE, SLAVE, DO WHAT YOU'RE TOLD, SLAVE
OR I SLAP YOUR BLACK FACE, I SLAP YOUR
BLACK FACE AND I KICK YOUR BLACK BELLY I
KICK YOUR BLACK BELLY AND KICK IT TILL IT
CAVES RIGHT IN AND IT CAN'T HOLD MORE
BABIES EVER AGAIN. NO MORE UGLY BLACK
BABIES THAT YOU'LL ... that you'll like more than
me. Even though I'm ten years old I made you die. I
made you go in that march and I made you die. I
know that forever. I said I was sorry, I'm sorry, I'm
sorry, I'm sorry, I'm sorry, but you never looked at me
again. You hated me. But I love you, Nellie, more than
Mummy or Daddy and I want you to come back, and
sing those songs, and roll mealie pap and be washing
the floor in your nice uniform so I can came in and ask
you to make a pink cake and your eyes will tickle me.
And you will say 'yes.'
'Yes, I'll make a pink cake....'

Tornado

Notes

Tornado was commissioned by the Canadian
Broadcasting Corporation for the radio series *Sextet*,
and was first broadcast on the CBC Stereo network
on November 29, 1987, with the following cast:

MANDY	Jennifer Dale
ROSE	Patricia Phillips
BILL	Geoff Bowes
JAKE	Noam Zilberman
JANE	Susan Coyne
SHIRLEY, JILL, PAM	Ann Holloway
COP, DAVID, DAD	George Buza
DR. SOY, JIM, BOB	Ray Landry
BARNEY, DOCTOR	Don Allison
RACHEL	Megan Smith
MARC, COP 2	Richard Binsley
SALLY	Diana Belshaw
JUNE, JOAN, MOM	Kate Hurman
ELLEN	Sandra Scott
JULIE	Marsha Moreau
JOE	Marlow Vella
JOHN 2	Finlay MacNeil
JOHN, WAITER	Frank Pellegrino

Produced and directed in Toronto and Vancouver by
John Juliani. Original music composed by Bill Skolnik,
performed by Dick Smith, Eugene Amaro and Bill
Skolnik. Sound effects prepared by Matt Willcott and
Joe Silva. Technical operations controlled by Glen
McLaughlin and Gene Loverock. Production
assistants: Nina Callaghan and Loretta Joyce.

Scene One

A very large noisy party – a summer barbecue.

SOUND *Party noise – especially an electric steak knife carving roast beef.*

JIM That's some piece of meat there, David.

DAVID My brother-in-law got it, you know, buys the whole bull, we got half in our freezer they got half in theirs.... It's the only way to do it.

SALLY Oh GOD I could never do that.

JILL The meat's delicious, David!

JIM Why not? Sounds like a –

JOHN *Great meat*, David.

SALLY Because then you'd *know* that you're eating an animal, you'd have a dead body in your freezer, I mean

DAVID Oh Jeez, you're not going macrobiotic on us, are ya Sal?

SALLY No, I think maybe it's just being pregnant, I'm more, you know

BARNEY Rachel McNaught! Did I just see you eat four devilled eggs!?

RACHEL You tell a soul and I'll murdalize you, Barney.

MANDY NO! No no no no NO I HATE CHILDREN. I DO NOT WANT A CHILD.

MARC DON'T tell me what when you see your friends suckling their beautiful little newborns you don't get at least a twinge?

MANDY I get nauseated, that's what I get, Marky, I'm telling you I am *not* a slave of biology.

JUNE Come on, Amanda. I have four children and I do not consider myself a slave.

MANDY WELL lady you are. You are a slave of your hormones. What does having kids get ya, huh? A lotta sleepless nights, a few cute snaps, and four ordinary stupid human beings the world could do without.

JUNE You're drunk, Amanda.

MANDY Just cause I don't want a little duplicate of me running around, a little CLOOONE....

Scene Two

In another room – BILL, *Mandy's husband, and* JANE, *his lover, talk.*

BILL I had to kiss you.

JANE OH ME TOO, ME TOO....

BILL [*they are kissing*] Oh GOD.

JANE Will you tell her? Will you tell her tonight?

BILL Yeah. Yeah, I will, yeah.

JANE Cause I've told Stephen.

BILL You did?

JANE As soon as he got home from work, I ... told him, I told him about you, I told him ... that ... I was moving out ... and I'm ... I'm in a hotel room at the Chelsea, I've moved out, you can come tonight after you've told her.

BILL Tonight.

JANE We can have a whole night together, finally, a whole

BILL Well, wait a minute, Jane, she might, you know Mandy, she'll want to talk about it all night, she

JANE Well just say no say NO, Bill, *Bill*

BILL [*silence*]

JANE Do you love me?

BILL You know I do.

JANE Do you want me?

BILL Okay tonight. I'll tell her tonight and then

JANE Room 456. I'll be awake, and

SHIRLEY [*pushes open the door*] Hi ya!

JANE Shirley!

SHIRLEY So – this is the den, is it?

JANE Yeah, we were just ... looking at this wonderful sculpture

BILL I ... believe they picked it up in Tanzania ... it's a fertility god or something.

SHIRLEY Bizarre that it's made of glass, isn't it? I mean most African sculptures are made of wood, aren't they?

JANE, BILL Yes, yes, I think so, yes they are....

SHIRLEY Bizarre that it's made of glass.

BILL So ... I'll be getting back to the party.... [*leaves*]

SHIRLEY Shoot, I'm sorry, did I interrupt a lover's –

JANE No no, well, kind of, but it was over.

SHIRLEY Has he told her?

JANE No.

SHIRLEY You should see her out there, she is tanked right up. No wonder he's frightened of her.

JANE He isn't frightened of her.

SHIRLEY She's his big mummy, Jane, that's why – [*drops glass thing*]

JANE Oh my GOD

SHIRLEY Uh oh....

JANE What are you going to do? That thing is priceless, it's

SHIRLEY We will just make our exit, making sure that we are not noticed. Stealth, get it? Okay? *Now.* [*party noise*]

Scene Two A

Move out of room.

JANE Oh my God if Hilda finds out she'll

SHIRLEY She won't find out. Now hush and tell me more.

JANE He's going to tell her tonight.

SHIRLEY That's what he said two months ago, Jane, the man's a *liar.*

JANE He is not he is not, Shirley – oh God I need some coke, get me some coke.

SHIRLEY Jane you do NOT need

JANE Where's Barney. BARNEEE.

SHIRLEY Janey, if Bill finds out you're a coke head, he'll

JANE He's not going to find out.

BARNEY You called?

JANE Barney I'm depressed.

BARNEY You want to go to the bathroom?

JANE Yes.

SHIRLEY JANE

JANE Bye Shirley.

BARNEY You can come too!

SHIRLEY NO thank you.

Scene Three

Outdoors.

BOB This beef is *fantastic.*

DAVE Yeah, well we froze a whole cow, you know, a bull, and

ELLEN I had a pedicure for the first time and you know, I really really enjoyed it!

JOAN Oh I couldn't live without them now.

MANDY SEVENTEEN! We met when we were seventeen, on CHERRY beach, I was on the beach with my girlfriends and there he was walking along IN THONGS AND I said to Pam, my best girlfriend, I said that is the man I am going to marry!

MARC Oh please, not that puke-making heterosexual mythology PLEASE

MANDY IT'S TRUE. And he looked at me with those EYES! I mean talk about EYES and we've been screwing since that very night!

PAM Charming.

MANDY BILEEEEE!! Bileee!

BILL You want me dear?

MANDY Time to go, buster, I gotta hit the hay.... *Serious.*

Scene Four

Fast food place.

GIRL Can I take your order sir?

BILL Yeah, two hamburgers, two vanilla shakes

MANDY No, chocolate, make mine chocolate.

BILL One vanilla one chocolate.

MANDY Burgers and shakes! Ohhh I'm a happy giiirrrl!!

84

Scene Five

A car drives up to a beautiful spot by the water.

MANDY Hey what's this, you want to watch the submarine races?

BILL Listen to the water!

MANDY Bill, come on, I'm exhausted....

BILL Just ... I just ... need to talk ... okay?

MANDY Talk, Christ, what about?

BILL I just ... I need to talk ... about ... us.

MANDY Well we're fabulous, what do you mean you need to talk about us?

BILL [*silence*]

MANDY Bill?

BILL I have to go outside, do you mind if we walk outside.

MANDY No.

SOUND *They get out.*

MANDY Well, will ya talk for Christ's sake – what's on your mind?

BILL I ... it's so hard to say.

MANDY Jesus that wind is strong out here, give me your sweater?

BILL Sure, sure, here.

MANDY Now talk, will you talk?

BILL I've ... I'm seeing somebody else. [*breaking down*] I ... I've ... been ... seeing

MANDY Who is it.

BILL I'm ... I'm not saying just yet. I just want to –

MANDY WHO IS IT?

BILL Jane ... Jane ... Coots.

MANDY JANE COOTS

BILL I ... I'm sorry, I –

MANDY Why

BILL I don't know, I never....

MANDY What can Jane Coots give you that I can't, BILLY? EH? EH? What can Jane Coots give you that I can't??

BILL Chi –

MANDY WHAT

BILL Chi-l-dren.

MANDY [*frightened*] Children ...?

BILL Yes. I – I ... want, I need ... children ... Mandy, I've decided that ... I want to have children.

MANDY You WANT to have children?

BILL ... more ... than anything.

MANDY Why ... why didn't you ... tell me, Bill

BILL Well, because you're always ... telling everybody how you hate children, how that's the last thing you –

MANDY I WAS LYING! I WAS LYING, BILL, DON'T YOU SEE?

BILL Lying? Why?

MANDY FOR YOU! For YOU because I thought YOU DIDN'T WANT

BILL Why ... why did you think that?

MANDY You never said! I wanted to let you off the hook. It's the way I was brought up; if a man doesn't mention something ... I ... I wanted to please you, Bill, I didn't want to pressure you ... I ... want ... a child, more than anything.

BILL You ... do? You really do?

MANDY A baby! Let's have a baby together. Okay? Okay?

BILL Well – yes! Yes!

MANDY Take me back to the car.

Scene Six

Later that night, in bed.

SOUND BILL *sleeping soundly.*

MANDY [*whispers*] Come on, sperm, come on, don't die, strike strike the egg, STRIKE! But if you fall out, fall out, turn into white worms, and crawl across the sheet, across the floor, over the wet streets grow poison fangs and crawl into JANE COOTS' bed over the sheets up to her temple, slide up to her temples and STRIKE STRIKE slide in the side of her head and chew on her brain. CHEW and CHEW till she screams out for mercy, till she screams and screams and then STRIKE!!

Scene Seven

JANE's *hotel room.*

JANE [*screams at the word 'strike' and wakes up, terrified, startled*] Oh God what a dream ... I must have a fever ... Aghh ... What time is it ... five thirty ... five thirty ... oh no. Oh no [*crying*] OHHH NO!

SOUND *Jane dials a number on the phone.*

JANE Shirley? It's Jane here, guess what? [*crying*] He didn't come! He didn't come!

Scene Eight

ROSE [*talking to us*] So, ya see, like, my Mum was good an everything like, she did everything, like she even tied my hair in rags, like for church and she stayed up all night sewin a green pinafore for like school, and I'd come in from neckin with a boy and she knew it, eh, she knowed, she wouldn't say tho, all's she'd say is 'have a good time dear?' and I'd blush beet-red and run to my room she was good. She was a hairdresser, formally. But my Daddy, now he's another story, it's like I never knew how she could be married to him, like, like he'd come in at night with a jar, right? And he'd say 'just want to pick the worms outa your behind, all you kids got worms in the behind, you just stay asleep' then I suddenly felt like a thunderbird, one of them thunderbird cars? Went right up my hooey like a car accident up in my hooey over and over a head-on collision and then after about a million hours where I bit my tongue almost in half dad'd say 'no worms there tonight' and all these white worms, white dead worms would fall outa my hooey see that's what I thought they was, since I was so little, I thought they was the worms he was lookin for, dead from the car crash. Course I know now that they wasn't worms, they was spermatozoa, like, come.

87

Then other nights he'd come in say 'open your mouth
wide Rosey rose, I gotta put a flashlight up there look
for mouth worms,' and 'keep your teeth tucked,' he'd
say, 'keep em tucked,' and then he'd put his light in
he'd say 'I can see the back of your throat honey Rose,
bright as anything,' and that light would keep going in
and in and I's gonna choke on it and then he pulled it
out I know now that that wasn't no flashlight neither.
So I want to have as many children as I can have so I
can love them the good way, the way my mummy
started lovin me before. So I got these kids, these four
kids, I love them more than my life more than your life
and this fifth one coming in five months ... See, this is
one thing I can do, I can do it some girls can't but I can
I can love them and I know how from my mum, see
how good they are they're good as, Julia, please get us
some more ice tea thank you?

JULIE Yes Mummy.

ROSE An she's so good, an they're all good, they don't cry or
nothin.

MANDY She is, she's a doll, Rose, you brought her up very
well.

ROSE I know babies, I know children.

MANDY But, Rosy, is the welfare enough? This is what I'm
trying to determine; you see, the government sends
me out to determine if what they give you is enough.
Okay? Can we go through your monthly expenses?

ROSE Okay, sure, I can ... make up, I mean I don't have
paper but well, rent is yeah, six hundred.

MANDY Well then you have one hundred fifty dollars left over
for the month.

ROSE Yeah.

MANDY Well that won't do

ROSE I buy cheap and you know, Salvation and food depot
and restaurants they got so much leftover stuff.

MANDY No no, this is no good at all. Sweetie, I'LL TELL YOU
SOMETHING, we are going to get you more for you
and your ... little ones. TELL ME, it says here that you
have epilepsy, is everything fine in that ... area? It's not
a worry with the kids?

ROSE Oh no, no, like I only have one like, maybe once a month, eh, just two minutes long, one two minutes.

JAKE One minute and twenty one seconds was the last, then she started gulpin

ROSE He means gulpin for air, see, I got him to time them, make sure the baby in my tummy's gettin enough air – it's only as big as a telephone receiver right now. He's a good timer, he's got his stopwatch his BIG BROTHER gave him, like not his real big brother cause he's the eldest but one of these college guys, takes him out to baseball games.

JAKE Concerts too, we went to AC-DC last week.

JULIE I timed one once, Mummy, forty-five seconds, bemember?

ROSE Of course I do, lamb.

MANDY Well, they're a great help, these kids.

ROSE And like I always feel when they're comin on, I get plenty of warning three four minutes, enough time to put the baby in the crib and lie down on the floor, tell the kids. They're just fine with it, they don't mind a BIT.

MANDY Well ... that's ... and the ... uh ... you are presently on medication?

ROSE Oh yes, I took em with all my kids, no trouble never ... cept one Julie there, she was born without no fingernails, but they grew didn't they Jul?

JULIE And my Mummy painted them pink!

ROSE She likes that.

MANDY WELL, that's, uh, I didn't realize that ... medications were alright.

ROSE Oh yeah all my kids is way smarter than me anyways.

MANDY WELL, Rose, it's been very nice to meet you, I should be on my way now, four more clients to see today. After this, though, I do think you might ... think about ... contraception, maybe even get your tubes tied after this baby ... or?

ROSE No, no, thank you, no. I'm goin to have as many babies as my belly will carry, cause they need me. All the unborn babies hangin out there in limbo, they need my hands to hold them and wash their little feet. I love

their feet, you know, more than any other part, I think
cause their feet, they're not feet like our feet are, they
could be anything else, they could be ... like ... a white
bird flyin away or some kinda white flower.
MANDY Well, I really do have to go ... Bye bye. Bye bye, kids.
CHORUS OF KIDS Bye. Bye lady. Bye bye.
ROSE Come on, come on Jake and let's get these monkeys
supper.

Scene Nine

Bill's office. Very noisy investment firm.

BILL [*on the phone*] Okay, I'll tell you what I'm going to do
for you, I'm going to buy you fifteen thousand shares
first thing tomorrow yeah, yes, it is very safe ... well
our analysts assure us that ... yes okay, alright, yes,
five minutes. [*hangs up, picks up another phone*] HELLO,
Octon Cave, and –
JANE [*filter*] Hello Bill.
BILL Jane, look, I'm ... I am sorry if we inconvenienced you
at all the other night – I've been trying to
JANE WE, Bill, why are you saying WE
BILL Jane, listen, let's meet and talk over dinner, how does
that sound?
JANE O.K. ... Bill? Is everything alright?
BILL Fine, everything is just fine, Jane. Now, where would
you like to meet?

Scene Ten

*Mandy's office: College Branch, Ministry of Community
and Social Services.*

RECEPTIONIST Good morning. Yes she is, would you hold on
please Bill? Mandy, Bill for you.
MANDY Got it. Hi handsome, what's up?
BILL [*filter*] We're meeting her at Doogles around seven, is
that okay for you?

MANDY Seven? Sure, I'm meeting with the Minister at five-thirty. I'm sure I'll be all wrapped up by seven. How did you like last night?

BILL Very much. How about you?

MANDY I think we made a baby.

BILL Yeah? What makes you think that?

MANDY My nipples are sensitive. Supposed to be a sure sign!

BILL Hey, I don't want it to be THAT easy.

MANDY YOU BEAST. Anyway, gotta run, see you at seven.

BILL Bye bye love.

Scene Eleven

MANDY'S BOSS So, did you find out anything today?

MANDY Oh Mr. BOSS man, yes! I found out that everybody needs more money. I have one lady, epileptic single mother, four kids another on the way, living on seven hundred fifty a month! Poor as shit and she's waxing on about how gorgeous is a baby's foot!

BOSS Well, put it all in your report, and we will sock it to the minister!

MANDY RIGHT. God, it's great to be in a job where ya feel useful. This beats the hell out of real estate, I'll tell you.

BOSS You made more money in real estate.

MANDY So I bought more gourmet pesto, I had my house cleaned more at fifteen bucks an hour, you know? Like, who cares?

Scene Twelve

JANE *and* SHIRLEY *in washroom.*

SHIRLEY I'm telling you, Janey, DON'T GO.

JANE I love the guy, Shirley.

SHIRLEY I KNOW it's going to be bad, from what you told me he's going to show up, and shuffle around and then ... boo hoo, can't leave the wife.

JANE NO. NO. I don't believe it, he's a GOOD man, he loves me.

SHIRLEY He has dirty water for blood, Jane, I've seen them
before. These soft-spoken gentle ones are the worst,
they feel nothing, they take responsibility for nothing,
like fish, they just let the water take them, BILLY IS A
BIG FISH, he's a SHIT!

JANE DON'T ... don't try to speak to me again today,
Shirley. I could get very mad at you.

SHIRLEY Okay, okay, I won't try to speak to you again. Okay.

Scene Thirteen

Busy restaurant. Jazzy music. MANDY *and* BILL *are
entering.*

MANDY Kind, but firm, got it?

BILL I'm afraid she won't like this....

MANDY Tough tahooties....

BILL JANE! I hope you don't mind, I brought Mandy
along....

JANE Ohh ohh well, I mean, I didn't expect....

MANDY Amazing I'm alive, eh, considering your concerted
attempt to annihilate

BILL Let's sit down, why don't we.

JANE I think ... I'm going to leave, I didn't want this kind of

MANDY Sit down Jane, I think you owe me this.

BILL Please?

JANE Well?

MANDY Listen to me. These are the facts. You moved in on our
marriage when it was at a crisis point – don't
interrupt, please – a crisis point that we arrived at
through our own stupidity. We know that now, we
have discussed that. In fact, we would like ... actually,
Jane, to thank you, for saving our marriage.

JANE Is this some kind of joke?

BILL Jane, Mandy and I ... we ... hadn't talked about some
very important things, we were both afraid

MANDY Terrified

BILL And ... my ... affair with you ... brought these things....

MANDY TO THE FORE

BILL To the fore

MANDY It's not a joke, honestly, we want ... it's very hard for me I'll admit, but I would even like to be friends with you.

BILL Sure, I mean, I like you, JANE.

JANE You said a lot more than that.

MANDY Jane, Bill has told me everything he ever said to you, so don't think

JANE Amanda, he may have told you everything, but don't think you know, don't think for a second that you can EVER know what went on between our ... faces, our mouths, you don't know.

BILL Please, Jane, of course I value our friendship.

JANE 'Affair,' Bill, we screwed, we screwed our brains out and we both said we could die happy after that, we both

MANDY I know all that, Jane, I told you, he told me EVERYTHING.

JANE How could you?

BILL Amanda is my wife, Jane, I ... I ... I was in a ... phase of a kind of self destructiveness, and you ... well you fit in

JANE Are you trying to tell me you ... used me?

BILL ... I'll never be able to forgive myself for it, but ... yes, I in my ... rampage against myself and the woman I love more than my life, you were ... a ... tool ... I'm ... I don't know how to tell you I'm sorry

JANE That's okay, that's okay, Bill, because, GOD, you guys, you two are really, I mean ... I don't believe you, see? I think she you, boy, lady, you, I sometimes think you're a witch, you know that? I think you....

MANDY WE didn't want to hurt you, Jane.

JANE No, no, that's fine, I mean, really, I think you are a witch, because I know this man, I know your husband far better than you could ever know him and I know that he ... I KNOW THAT YOU LOVE ME, BILL, I know that you were not ... lying, or

BILL I have *a great* love for your ... spirited way of....

JANE NO, no, screwing love, Bill, man woman *only* love. I know, [*she is crying now*] I KNOW

MANDY There's no need to cause a scene, honey.

JANE YES THERE IS! Oh yes. [*She pulls off the tablecloth, everything shatters, crowd reacts*] Oh yes there is.

MANDY Let's leave, Bill.

JANE THIS WOMAN IS A WITCH SHE IS A WITCH, SHE PUT A HEX ON MY MAN SHE PUT A CURSE.

BILL [*to* WAITER] Here's sixty dollars for any damages. I'm sorry.

WAITER Lady, listen

JANE [*attacks* MANDY] I'LL KILL YOUUUUUU! I'll kill youuuuuu!!

MANDY Let go of me ... Helllp! Billeeee help!

BILL Help. Somebody help!

JANE I'll friggin rip your eyes out, you evil witch, you evil evil

MANDY Help me!

OTHERS Fight, fight, hey look at the two broads goin at it.

OTHER Oh I love it, over that wimpy looking guy? Can you believe it?

JANE I'll killll you
[*Men wrestle her away*]
I'll kill youuuuu

MANDY I suppose you know that assault is a punishable offence.

JANE I don't care! I don't care! I'll killll – [*drops to floor sobbing*] Oh GOD oh GOOOOOD

SHIRLEY JANEY? [*spits*] You pigs, have you done this?

MANDY Let's go, Billy. Listen, Jane,
[JANE *is sobbing wildly*]
I know you feel a great deal of hostility towards us now, I know, believe me, and it's understandable but I want you to know, that we do want to be your friends, we would like, WOULDN'T WE BILL, WE ... would very much like to have you to dinner ... sometime....

JANE [*screams*] Get out!

BILL Let's go, love.

SHIRLEY Oh Janey Janey Janey, that fish.

Scene Fourteen

ROSE's *place.*

SOUND   *Cartoons in background.*

JULIE   And what else do you miss from the country mummy?

ROSE   Gimme another sip of that iced tea, Jujube – mmn – that's nice –

JOE   Wha else

JAKE   The lobsters!

ROSE   No no, there weren't no lobsters there, just well, I told you the big trees we could climb, all the big trees

JOE   There's a tree just down the street, in the park.

ROSE   Yeah yea but not like our trees, our trees were real real special in the spring? like in the spring? They'd spill all this green fairy spray all over the sidewalk

JOHN 2   I seen that here, Mum.

ROSE   And the sweat, like in the summer

JOE   I hate the summer here.

JULIE   I can't even sleep it's so hot, sometime.

ROSE   Well there, it was beautiful, cause you'd work on the Smithers farm all day, real hard, pickin up hay or whatever and you'd work up this sweat just pourin down, drippin on down your knees, your nose –

JULIE   Ewww

ROSE   Oh nooo, it was nice, you'd lay right down in the cool barn and fall dark asleep, just dark

JOE   I want to see a barn!

ROSE   Uh oh.

JAKE   Whatsa matter mum

ROSE   I feel ... I think ... oh boy, I think one's comin on, kids.

JULIE   Mummy!

JAKE   It's okay, it's okay. You kids settle down, Mum's gonna be –

ROSE   Jakey take the kids in the other room, you, kids, you kids watch the TV.

JAKE   [*quick*] Come on kids, let's go see cartoons

95

JOE I want to stay with mumeeee

ROSE Jakey!

JAKE Come on! NOW COME ON!!

KIDS I don't want to. No.

SOUND JAKE *shuts door and rushes back in to* ROSE.

JAKE Come on! I got the stopwatch, ma.

ROSE Oh no, God, things are starting to –

JAKE It's okay Ma, I'm here, won't let nothin happen to ya, turn on your side now

[ROSE *goes into seizure*]

S'okay Mum s'okay ... you think you're on the other side of the dark but I'm holding onto ya I'll bring ya back, I know I know, I can see what it's like, I can see it ma, I can see you're turning upside down and around a million million times and as fast as inside a dryer and falling and faster and faster and ice picks and scissors and snakes and every sick sound like throwin up and crushin eggs and mean laughin and everybody's laughin and you're fallin, I know, fallin fallin so fast so fast and you're at the bottom you're at the bottom now covered with mud and if you don't breathe if you don't breathe the light will be covered with mud, black, covered with mud if you don't breathe you'll be dead underground, COME ON, COME ON, YOU CAN SEE IT, you can see it at the top, *TRY* I'm here, your Jakey's here, so just scream, just scream mummy, scream your scream out and you'll fly to the top burst through the air let the scream take ya let it carry ya up bang! through to the air

ROSE [*screams a blood-curdling scream*]

SOUND *Sounds of TV heard and the kids crying 'Mummy.'*

JAKE It's okay, everybody, she's screamin up! She's screamin up!

JULIE She's screamin up!

JOHN, JOE She's okay?

ROSE [*a loud blood-curdling scream again, followed by about four intense bursts of scream*]

Scene Fifteen

Outside Rose's door.

SOUND *The door, which was open a bit, swings open. It is* MANDY.

MANDY Rose? Rose? Out of the way, please. Rose ... are you....

ROSE Oh Jesus.

JAKE She got took, that's all, she got took on the other side but I brung her back, it's okay, it's

ROSE A small fit, that's all, just a little

MANDY Where are the other children?

JOE Mummy?

JAKE I took care of em, it's okay. They was watchin TV, it's okay, lady, just

ROSE Jakey

MANDY Are you ... alright now? Would you like me to call an ambulance?

ROSE Oh no, no thank you. I don't want a bunch of twenty-one-year-old kids pokin their hands in me, no no, I'm okay, I'm just fine, I'll just finish ... supper.

MANDY Don't you think you had better ... lie down ... or ... would you like me to see about Homemakers, or

ROSE No, no, if you don't mind, I'd just like to fix my kids supper, I got fish thawin there and....

MANDY I ... I just came to tell you that we ... got the money.

ROSE Money?

MANDY One hundred and seventy-five more dollars a month more ... I know it's nowhere near what you need, but....

ROSE We could use it.

JOE Mummy I want a cookie, Mum? I want a cookie

ROSE Joe! DO YOU ... want a cup of tea ... or....

MANDY No, no, I won't bother you, I just – I just wanted to bring the good news ... I ... hope you're feeling better ... You look great –

ROSE When is the money?

MANDY Within six to eight weeks, I'll ... bring it to you....

ROSE Glad ... I'm glad ... Julie? Would you please set the table ... John, Joey, get in your seats, please.

MANDY   Anyway I'll ... I'll be in touch.
ROSE   Yeah.
SOUND   MANDY *leaves.*

Scene Sixteen

Doctor's office: Mandy's obstetrician drops the bad news.
DR. SOY   And you see these little hairs, or cilia normally brush
that egg down the tube and into the uterine lining, just
like, say, curling! Sweeping the rock, or whatever it's
called, but when we did the exploratory surgery we
found, in your case –
MANDY   DON'T TELL ME ANYMORE I DON'T WANT TO
KNOW ANYMORE
DR. SOY   There are other options, Mrs. Swain.
MANDY   Like what, what? If you've got blocked tubes you're
screwed, everyone knows –
DR. SOY   Well, in vitro
MANDY   What?
DR. SOY   In glass, literally.
MANDY   Oh test tube, sure, one out of two hundred or
something no, no, I don't know. OH shit. I don't
know, I just ... I just want to go home.
DR. SOY   If you change your mind....
MANDY   I just ... want to go home.

Scene Seventeen

Mandy's house.
SOUND   MANDY *opens the door to her home.*
MANDY   Helloooo, I'm hooome.
   [BILL *and* JANE *walk towards her*]
BILL   Amanda! Jane just dropped in for
MANDY   I'm sorry, I wasn't ... expecting anybody.

BILL   I was just home picking up a case file and she
      happened

JANE   I was just ... going for a walk and I remembered you'd
      said to ... drop in anytime, so I....

MANDY   If you'll excuse me, I have to go upstairs and lie down,
      I'm not feeling very well. Bill? I'd appreciate some tea
      in a while, if you don't mind. Camomile.

BILL   Sure, sure, the kettle's on right now, as a matter of
      fact.

JANE   We were just going to have a second cup.

MANDY   If you'll excuse me ...
      [MANDY *goes up the stairs. There is a moment of silence*]

JANE   She knows.

BILL   No, no, I don't think so.

JANE   Then why was she so....

BILL   She's just been to the doctors ... she ... probably got ...
      bad news. I should....

JANE   Look at you, as soon as she comes in you're a
      different....

BILL   Jane

JANE   Billy I could have a baby for you like THAT – I got
      pregnant every time Steve even looked at me. I could
      give you as many children as you want. I know how
      much you –

BILL   Shhhhh. I think you'd better go.

JANE   So what, Bill, she probably knows, this whole house
      reeks of sex.

BILL   Gooo *now*.

Scene Eighteen

MANDY   [*from listening place; to herself*] Oh GOD oh GOD my
      Bill don't leave me I'll – make a baby for you I will –

BILL   Man? Do you want milk in your tea?

MANDY   [*startled*] No thanks love ... Is Jane still

BILL   No no, she's left ... she just wanted to talk about
      boyfriend problems.

MANDY Ohhh I see. Poor Jane.
BILL Yeah. Poor Jane.
MANDY Billy? Come here and kiss me.
BILL [*kisses her*] I'll to get your tea. [*he goes out*]
MANDY Oh God ... Take me to the other side, seize my body and my blood – hot wind cold wind, TAKE ME INTO THE FIT, whip – my – body and my brain – bring me a baby! [*teeth chatter loudly*] Take me down into the dark, down into the – [*release*] Oh LORD, LORD Ohhh yes!

Scene Nineteen

Rose's place. Noise of kids playing. TV on. Rainy day outside.
SOUND *Knocking on door.*
ROSE Coming! Coming!! Jakey would you get it mummy's just on the john.
JAKE Okayyyy! Who's there.
MANDY It's Mrs. Swain? The social worker from the Ministry with your check.
JAKE Mumm, it's the one with those great big hands and red lips. Should I let her in?
ROSE [*flushing*] Jakey don't you be so rude! [*she unlatches door*] I'm sorry ... he's just ... you know, seven ... boy, you look drenched to the bone!
MANDY Yes, it's just slamming down, like being SHELLED.
ROSE My Dad was in the war. Come in, you'll have to excuse the mess.
MANDY Oh GOD, you should see my place sometimes.
ROSE Oh, I'm sure it's as neat as a pin.
MANDY ANYWAY, Rose, I have brought you your check!
ROSE Well, it took long enough!
MANDY That's why I decided to bring it in person. You know how the mail is.
ROSE WELL that's so nice of you would you like some – tea?
MANDY Thank you, I would, thank you.
ROSE Okay, would – plain be –
JULIE I'll do it Mum

JAKE No way, you're too little, let me....

JOHN No, me

JOE I want to do it

ROSE Julie asked first. Julie will do it; you kids into the bedroom while I'm talkin to the lady. I think Mr. Dressup is on. Me and the social worker has to chat for a while.

JOHN But I want to see her big hands

JULIE Could I borrow your lipstick

ROSE Childs! Into the bedroom please, and now! Jakey could you

JAKE No prob, Mum, okay, soldiers, march! *Hup* two three four, hup two three four

JULIE, JOE One two

JOHN One two three six

SOUND *Door closes.*

MANDY They're really sweet.

ROSE They are ... sweet....

MANDY Yes, that's ... evident ... well ... so, how are you feeling?

ROSE A little tired.

MANDY Rose, I have some ... rather .. shocking news relating to your condition –

ROSE None of the children are epileptic so far, so don't try to tell me

MANDY No, no, it's not that, it's a very surprising ... study they have just completed in Montreal, Vancouver, and independently in Japan and France. [*clearing throat*] Rose, these studies prove that in the case of epileptic women having their fourth or fifth child ... that invariably, well, in ninety-seven cases out of one hundred, when they bring that child home, the child, well, the child ... invariably ... dies.

ROSE What!? Nobody ever – why?

MANDY Nobody really knows, it's a sudden infant death syndrome, you know, the infant is simply found dead in its crib.

ROSE Their heart – stopped?

MANDY No, their ... brains ... seem to stop functioning and these scientists say that it seems to be a result not of genetic flaws but of close contact with the mother –

ROSE Why would that be, the breast –

MANDY No no, it happens even in the case of bottle-fed babies, some of the scientists have theorized that [*cough*] Excuse me, that there is a virus, carried by the mother, that could in fact be responsible for her epilepsy, that is passed to the child through the mother's sweat

ROSE Through her sweat?

MANDY Seems incredible, doesn't it?

ROSE Through her sweat?

MANDY Well many viruses, such as the AIDS virus have been found in sweat and tears

ROSE Oh no.

MANDY I'm afraid that these studies are so conclusive that the Minister of Health has ordered us to go into the community and ... inform women such as yourself of the situation and help them ... to find a suitable place for the baby ... After all you wouldn't want ... the baby to die

ROSE How come my doctor never

MANDY These studies have just been released, Rose, two days ago

ROSE You're saying I'll have to give up the child?

MANDY Rose, there are many wonderful, wealthy, brilliant couples just dying, dying for a child. Your baby will bring them such happiness.
[ROSE *is crying*]
NOW, very important, you mustn't breathe a word of this to anybody else, NOBODY

ROSE Why not? My social worker –

MANDY Rosy, it's top secret and the punishment for violation of Government secrets is life in prison. How would that be for your kids!

ROSE Bastards!

MANDY Now look, you have ... when exactly are you due?

ROSE Now, well, yesterday....

MANDY I want you to call me as soon as you go into labour. I'll go to the hospital with you as your social worker. I have the right forms, and then as soon as you deliver, if everything's alright, I'll take the baby and you'll never have to even see –

ROSE My Dad was right, there isn't a God, there couldn't be, to let such –

MANDY The baby's life will be saved, Rose!

ROSE The baby's life will be – saved –

MANDY So, if you'll just sign your name here ... you can sign your name?

Scene Twenty

BILL *and* JANE *in motel room.*

BILL Oh GOD, I've never had one like that. My knees are like rubber! HOLD ME tighter Ohh –

JANE Me too, me too ... oh ... baby, baby, we *have* to be together we just have to

BILL I know I *know now* – oh – it's just not *like* this with her.

JANE You've got to just ... tell her the truth

BILL I know

JANE Bill!

BILL I know

JANE Did you hear me

BILL Yes, yes, I heard you

JANE You're still afraid of her, aren't you? Even with me carrying your child, you're afraid to leave her. What – IS the hold she has on you? What is it? She's not beautiful, she's not particularly intelligent

BILL I don't know. She ... I just couldn't ... let her down when she's so fragile, I –

JANE Well what about me? What about our

BILL Be quiet. Please. Just for now. Be quiet. Touch me there.

Scene Twenty-one

MANDY *and* BILL *at their home eating dinner. Jazz on stereo.*

BILL But honey, don't those ... women often change THEIR MINDS AT THE LAST minute?

MANDY Not this one, no way.

BILL How can you be so sure?

MANDY Let's just say I'd bet you a million dollars, okay? I'm one hundred percent sure. One hundred percent.

BILL Well, that's great! A baby in the house! Yahoo!

MANDY Yahoooo! Ohh [*hugs him*]

BILL When ... when is this baby supposed to....

MANDY Any time now ...! Really! Could be tonight!

BILL And all the legal work's been

MANDY EVERYTHING done, this guy's AMAZING OHHHH! Turn the music up!
[*She turns it up. They have to shout*]

BILL What was her fee?

MANDY Oh very low, just three thousand, I took it out of my account.

BILL That's very low, isn't it usually ten thousand?

MANDY No, that's only in the States! C'mere! I WANNA DANCE! Mandy wants to dance! [*she turns the music up louder*]

Scene Twenty-two

Rose's home. ROSE *is having contractions. Making sounds. Phone.*

JAKE Mum ... I think you should go to the hospital now, I think.

ROSE No, no, Jake, not till the last

JAKE But you look bad, Ma, let me call you a cab

104

ROSE   Ooohh ... kay, ... okay, I guess there's no point in ...
       Jakey! Call this number first
JAKE   Who's that?
ROSE   That's ... the social worker with the big hands
JAKE   What for?
ROSE   Just call her, please. Her name is Mrs. Swain.
       Pleaseee
SOUND JAKE *dials number. It rings.*
MANDY [*filter*] Hello?
JAKE   Hello Mrs. Swain? My mum wants to talk to you.
       But be fast, she isn't feelin too good
MANDY Hello Rose
ROSE   It's comin, Mrs. Swain, I'm ... I'm goin to the
       hospital
MANDY Southwestern, right?
ROSE   That's right, Southwestern, maternity ward, Doctor
       Scott
MANDY You've informed Doctor Scott of your decision
       to give the baby up?
ROSE   Uhhh yes. Yes I did.
MANDY Good. I'll be there within the hour.

Scene Twenty-three

Delivery room. Sounds of a baby being delivered.
NURSE   A girl! You've got a beautiful baby girl!
ROSE   Is – she –
NURSE   Perfect! She's perfect! [*lots of cooing*]
ROSE   Take me away, take me away please! NOW! RIGHT
        NOW!!
NURSE   Okay, hon.
        [ROSE *is taken away*]
NURSE 2 She's giving it up, poor lady.
ANAESTHETIST Oh – I see.

Scene Twenty-four

Hospital room.

NURSE Sure ... Oh don't cry, Rose, you did good, you did real good

ROSE My Baby

MANDY Excuse me, I'd like to speak with Rose, please

NURSE Alright, five minutes.

MANDY Rose, she's just beautiful and you are doing a very very brave THING! Now remember, not another word!

ROSE I tell them, I'm one of those ... those surrogate girls

MANDY That's right, that's what they all think and that's the best thing for everyone. Remember. Treason is considered a far greater crime than even murder in this country!

ROSE Oh God

MANDY Goodbye Rose – I'm coming back in three days to pick up the baby. I won't stop in again so as not to upset you.

ROSE [*crying, after* MANDY'*s exit*] What did I do? What did I do to get this from ya, God, what?

Scene Twenty-five

MANDY *and* BILL'*s.*

SOUND *As* MANDY *walks in with the baby,* BILL *puts on Sharon Lois and Bram and/or blows horns and throws streamers. His* MOTHER *and her parents are also there.*

ALL Yayyy! Welcome!! Welcome Jennifer!! Let's see ... ohhh she's beautiful ... BEAUTIFUL!

MANDY Not too close, she's only three days old!

MUM Oh Manda, she's straight from heaven!

MANDY We're very lucky, Mum.

BILL   She is ... beautiful.
MANDY   She's ours!
DAD   Hi there, monkey!
BILL   Ohhh. Boy ... Hellooo Jenny ... this is your dad! This is
        your dad here! Ohh look at those blue blue eyes!
MANDY   I'm just gonna take her on up to her cradle and rock
        her a while
MUM   Shall I make you some tea, dear?
MANDY   No, no thanks mum, I don't need anything.

Scene Twenty-six

Hospital room. ROSE *is crying.* JAKE *is there holding her.*

JAKE   But mummy I don't get it, I just ... I don't ... get it!
        Why did the lady take the baby away?
ROSE   Because ... just because ... I ... I didn't think I could ...
        care for it.
JAKE   No way, Maa, I heard. I heard what she said. She said
        to you that bull about the fourth and fifth babies
        dying.
ROSE   You heard that?
JAKE   I didn't want to say nothin to get you mad.
ROSE   OK Jakey. Jakey we can't tell nobody or we go to jail
JAKE   Jail?
ROSE   For life! For....
DOCTOR So! Hello! Got the little ones here, I see, how are ya,
        young fellow?
JAKE   Doctor, just out of curiosity like I was wondering
ROSE   No Jake
JAKE   If the fifth babies of epileptics always die
DOCTOR Good heavens where'd you hear that nonsense, a TV
        show?
JAKE   The social worker
ROSE   JAKEY!! Jakey, nooo, we'll go to jail, we'll go to jail
        forever, for –
DOCTOR Rose? Is there something that I should know?

Scene Twenty-seven

MANDY *and* BILL*'s.*
SOUND *Baby's breathing.*
MANDY Awww, look at her mouth! Look at her mouth! She's ... beautiful. Do you love us, Bill? Do you love the baby and your wife?
BILL Oh yes, ohhh yes, more than anything – else!
MANDY Forever? For – ever – Bill?
SOUND *Phone rings.*
BILL I'll get it love. HELLO
JANE [*filter*] Billy, I'm sorry to call you there, but
BILL I'm sorry, there's no Ralph here, that's okay, bye –
JANE Bill! No Bill please I....
SOUND BILL *hangs up phone.*

Scene Twenty-eight

SHIRLEY What'd he say?
JANE He just ... pretended it was someone else. How am I going to reach him? I haven't been able to reach him for a week!
SHIRLEY Ohh he'll get in touch. I mean, what could have happened in a week? Come on, let's go sit down, you're looking green....

Scene Twenty-nine

Hospital room.
ROSE And she got me to sign some papers.
COP Oh boy, didn't you read them?
ROSE I can't read, really, just signs, the ladies room and that, Officer
COP She really did a number on you, boy

WORKER [*comes in*] Sergeant, we've tracked her down through the Ministry. Got her address right here.

COP Well, let's go then. You just sit tight, Mrs. Lamb, we'll get your baby back for you.

DOCTOR I JUST WISH you'd told me.

ROSE Life in the penitentiary, I thought my kids....

DOCTOR I know, I know ... some people.

Scene Thirty

Mandy's place. Music on, soft. They are dancing. MANDY *sings.*

MANDY When we're out together dancing cheek to cheek....

BILL How long to we have till next feeding?

MANDY Ohhh about forty-five minutes ... why, Mr. Swain? Did you have something – in mind?

SOUND *Front doorbell rings – one of those very dramatic rings.*

MANDY I wonder who that could be?

BILL Ohh probably Jehovah's Witnesses or something ... I'll get it.

MANDY Ohh don't answer it.

BILL Ohh

SOUND *Doorbell rings again.*

BILL I'll just send them away

MANDY Bill ... please....

SOUND *Now the police knock.*

COPS Open up. POLICE.

BILL Police! I wonder what

MANDY Oh probably something to do with those wild kids down the street. Would you take care of it, love, I'm just gonna go to the bathroom.

SOUND BILL *walks to the door and opens it.*

BILL Yes?

COP Mr. Swain?

BILL Yes

COP We have reason to believe that your wife has, in her possession, the child of one Mrs. Rose Lamb, is that correct?

BILL Well we have a child, yes, but it's all entirely legal, I
assure you, I saw the
SOUND MANDY *running down stairs.*
COP Sir, we have reason to believe your wife used fraud
and coercion to get that child, we have here –
COP 2 Does your wife own a blue station wagon, sir?
BILL Yes, what....
COP 2 Let's go.

Scene Thirty-one

MANDY *driving like a maniac in her car.*
SOUND *Much honking of horns, etc., throughout the speech.*
MANDY IT'S OKAY, BABY. THEY ARE NOT GONNA TAKE
YOU AWAY FROM ME IT'S ALL LEGAL,
EVERYTHING'S SIGNED ... ohhh God, the way you
look at me, you know I'm your real mummy, I'm your
real real Mummy cause I'm the one who WANTS you
more than anything I'm the one who thought about
you every second I would have grown you in my
tummy if I could, I tried, I tried but you had to grow in
another lady's tummy, yes! Yes my little apricot!! I
had mouldy soil, mouldy cilia they wouldn't sweep,
they wouldn't sweep, they were broken and mouldy,
mouldy. [*make up song*] Jenny Jenn – you are my peach
... my little nut, my little sweet, you are my cloud ... my
own.... [*sobbing*] Oh God Oh GOD they can't they
cannot take you no nooooo
SOUND *She screeches to a halt, takes the baby, slams the door.*

Scene Thirty-two

Outside at Cliff side.
MANDY Those nasty police cars won't be able to catch us
NOW cause on foot we can go anywhere and we can
hide in a box even or even even in the sewer, we can

hide for days and then and then we'll hitchhike to Alaska and I'll be a cancan dancer and build igloos and we can spear ... fish ... ANYTHING. Ohhh Jenny Jenn, people are lookin at us funny, did I forget to wear a bra? Or is my stocking run? Too much makeup on – maybe I look crazy, well I'm not, I'm not, don't you think it Jenn, I just want what is mine, you are mine and nobody nobody can take you, mine mine mine mine mine

BILL MANDY!!

MANDY GET AWAY FROM US!!

BILL Man ... please come away from the cliff honey, please? For me?

MANDY NO NO you all go AWAY SHE IS MINE SHE IS MYYY BABY

COP Take it easy, take it reallll easy, I've seen a few go over these bluffs –

BILL I love youu Mandy

MANDY No you don't, no you don't, this ... this is the exact spot where you told me you didn't love me, you don't ... want me anymore, you don't want me cause I am a cow – you want that skinny bitch, you don't want Jenny and me....

BILL Mandy, that's all over, I just want you, my wife, I

MANDY Nine months! Nine months I carried this child in my belly, I threw up every day for the first five and then I couldn't sleep for the last four months? And I kept fainting. All to bring your baby, your baby into the world, AND NOW YOU'RE TRYING TO TAKE HER AWAY FROM ME JUST BECAUSE I'M EPILEPTIC, WELL, I CAN'T HELP IT! I CAN'T HELP IT IF I GO TO THE OTHER SIDE, HOW DARE YOU, HOW DARE YOU

ROSE Mrs. Swain!

MANDY I'll kill us both, I swear, I'll keep my baby, dead or alive I'll jump, I'll kill us

COP Mrs. Lamb, I think she means it. YOU'D BETTER

JAKE Lady with the big hands!

MANDY I have big hands ... to hold a baaby, to calm a little

JAKE Lady can I talk to you?

ROSE Jakey no, for God's sake

JAKE Lady with the hands?

MANDY Yuh ... yes, okay, you ... you can bring me a sweater, nice boy, I'm I'm so cold, I'm so cold my teeth are chattering hear them the whole world can hear them they can hear them in Tanzania in ... I need ... a warmm ... sweater for me and my little ... baby ... I need

JAKE I'll bring it, lady, let me bring it?

MANDY Okay, okay ... but no one else. No one else or I'll jump!

JAKE Okay Mum?

COP What do you think Sergeant?

SERGEANT Yuh. Yes, okay ... who knows ... his voice seemed to calm her. Okay kiddo. But remember ... don't touch the baby, and don't say nothing that might make her mad or hurt her feelings got it?

ROSE Oh Jakey's real good that way ... he never says nothing to hurt nobody, he's real kind

SERGEANT Okay then, son ... go on

JAKE Okay....

BILL Here's a sweater....

JAKE I'm comin, lady! I'm comin with the sweater for ya! Don't jump or nothin

MANDY I'm ... so cold....

SOUND *The baby is crying throughout.*

MANDY It's okay, Jenny penny, it's okay, your mummy's here, she's here

JAKE Here's a sweater

MANDY It's Bill's

JAKE He wanted me to give it to you. To keep ya warm

MANDY I'll put it over the baby.

JAKE I can tell you love that baby

MANDY [*sobs*] YOU ... CAN?

JAKE I can tell ... that you're the kind of person who would do a high divin act, anythin ... to save that baby

MANDY Nobody seems to know that, they all think [*sobbing*] see, everybody I know thinks I'm such a selfish, awful ... and now they all think I'm even worse, they [*the baby cries*] It's okay, Jenn

JAKE No no, lady, no ... they know the truth about you now. They know that you have ... that you been on the other side

MANDY The ... other?

JAKE That you got taken ... just like my mum and her fits, you got taken by something that was bigger than yourself and that fit that takes can make for bad in the world sometimes but also for the – bestest, most greatest human – bean – acts ... they know ... that you ... are a great human act

MANDY I am?

JAKE You didn't mean to hurt nobody. You just wanted to care for a little one –

MANDY You know! You understand!

JAKE I knew from the moment I seen ya! And our family loves ya cause you brung us more money so we could have the cable some shoes for my mum you got a red mouth, from bitin your lip cause you want you want ... so much to care for a baby, I know!

MANDY I do, I love ... your baby, I ... love your little sister

JAKE And you can come visit anytime, and take her out, you can be like her big sister!

MANDY I could? You wouldn't ... throw me out of the house?

JAKE You can be GODmother to my little sister. How's that? I declare you fairy godmother. Do doooo! [*musical sound*]

MANDY You ... do?

JAKE Can I hold your big hand?

MANDY Thank you. Thank you. It's okay Jennifer.

COP It ... looks like ... he's doin okay....

ROSE He's some boy, Jakey, like a saint – don't know where he got it, not from his grandfather, that's for sure

BILL Look at that, he's leading her back, in one hand, and holding the baby in the other!

JAKE And you can bring us toys every week, and take us to light shows

MANDY [*still shivering, sobbing*] They won't hate me?

JAKE No ... cause you been to the other side.

MANDY ... but my ... husband ... he ... he doesn't

JAKE Him? He can't even grow a beard! Looks like weeds!
NO. Mandy, we're your husband now, our family

SOUND *Cry of baby, muffled sound of the cops, etc. converging on them.*

ROSE My baby my baby – my – oh – oh – what's –
happening – what's –

SOUND *The muffled sound becomes louder and louder although still muffled.* AMANDA's *breathing becomes fast, terrified, and then through it we hear* JAKE.

JAKE Amanda, Amanda, you have to breathe, if you don't breathe if you don't breathe the light will be covered with mud, black covered with mud if you don't breathe you'll be DEAD underground, COME ON, COME ON, YOU CAN SEE IT, you can see it at the top, *TRY* I'm here, your Jakey's here, so just scream, just scream Amanda, scream your scream out and you'll fly to the top burst through the air let the scream take ya let it carry ya up bang! through to the air.

I Am Yours

Notes

I Am Yours was first produced by the Tarragon
Theatre in Toronto on November 17, 1987, with
the following cast:

TOILANE Geordie Johnson
DEE Nancy Palk
MERCY Clare Coulter
MACK Peter Donaldson
RAYMOND William Webster
PEGS Patricia Hamilton

Directed by Derek Goldby.
Sets and lighting designed by Jim Plaxton.
Costumes designed by Melanie Huston.
Stage managed by Bruce McKinnon.

Characters

TOILANE
DEE
MERCY her sister
MACK Dee's husband
RAYMOND
PEGS Toilane's mother

Act One, Scene One

The stage is dark. TOILANE *walks slowly toward the audience, on a ramp that juts out into the audience. He is his six-year-old self, in a dream he is having as an adult. He is walking up to what he sees as a giant door, the door of his own home.*

TOILANE Mum! Muum, I'm home!
Hey, Mum, I'm home!
Where's my mummy?
But this is my house! I live here. [*pause*]
I do so! I do so live here! I do so live here! [*pause*]
I do so! My parents are in there! I do so live here, they're in there! I do live here, I do live here! I do live here! I do live here!
[*The 'door' slams. The audience should serve as the door. Do not bring in a real one.*]

Act One, Scene Two

MERCY, *on a bus, on her way to visit* DEE, *her sister, sitting next to a stranger, is having the same dream, about herself walking up to that door. She startles awake from the slam of the door.* DEE, *in her apartment, has also been having the same dream, but she can be standing, willing 'the creature' that torments her imagination to stay behind the wall, and not enter her being.*

MERCY I knew I shouldnta had that garlic chicken!

DEE There is nothing behind the wall. There is nothing behind the wall.

MERCY Did you ever wake up, well not quite wake up and you can't remember where you are? I mean just now, I thought I was in my old room at home, where I grew up, and then I wake up and I'm on this bus, I mean it's weird, on Highway Number One, in this dirty old bus, sitting next to a stinking, sleeping old Italian man who keeps leaning on me.

119

Act One, Scene Three

The same time. An October night, about three a.m. DEE *is feeling faint, needs air, and rushes downstairs to the courtyard where* TOILANE *is leaning against the wall. He stares at her.*

TOILANE ... Nice night.

[DEE *turns away.* DEE *starts to go*]
Hey hey do you ... do you not know who I am?

DEE [*shakes her head*] No...

TOILANE I'm the new super. You know, like the superintendent? So I'll be looking out for ya, right? Fixin your leaky taps, got a problem with the toilet, whatever! The name's Creese. Toilane Creese [*he extends his hand*] and you go by the name Deirdrena I believe, don't ya?

DEE Dee.

TOILANE Oh sure, I can call ya Dee, I'm not formal ...

DEE How do you know my name?

TOILANE ... the lists, the old super give me a list.

DEE Excuse me. [*she starts to go*]

TOILANE Hey! You got the most beautiful feet! I been meaning to tell ya I like the way they're so long ... must be size ten, eleven, eh?

[DEE *runs away*]
I like the way they're so long!

Act One, Scene Four

MERCY *is asleep on the bus. The stranger sitting next to her is an Italian labourer. He is sleeping.* MERCY *has the dream that follows and in her dream, he becomes* RAYMOND, *an older man who once picked her up hitchhiking and became her lover. In the blackout before this scene begins, James Brown's 'Prisoner of Love' should play, from the beginning, starting very loud.* RAYMOND *is bringing a rather guilty*] [*fifteen–year-old* MERCY *to orgasm by manipulating her vagina. She has an orgasm, and then immediately pretends that nothing at all has happened.*

MERCY God. I love that song.

RAYMOND It's a pleasant one ... not like that 'headache' music my kids play night and day.

MERCY [*flirting*] What's wrong, doncha like rock and roll?

RAYMOND It gives me ... a headache! [*they kiss*] Your lips taste like cough drops.

MERCY [*holds them up*] Want one?

RAYMOND No thank you, no good for the tummy.

MERCY I'm up to fourteen a day, no kidding, yesterday I had fourteen, in a row!

RAYMOND In a row!

MERCY In geography, I mean I was bored almost to death. I mean who cares about the Panama Canal, like who cares that ships can barely get through, like who gives a shit? Anyways, I gotta....

RAYMOND Mercia,

MERCY Yo!

RAYMOND I – I – I – wanted to give you – this.

MERCY A locket!

RAYMOND I – I – you'll notice the inscription.

MERCY An *inscription*; fuck, this musta cost you a mint – what's it say? 'Ich' – it's German!

RAYMOND Yes, it's – read it.

MERCY I can't read German.

RAYMOND Read it, go on. Try.

MERCY Okay. 'Ich' – that's 'ich' right? Ich – bin – dein? What's it mean?

RAYMOND It means –

MERCY SHIT. My garter belt, shit!

RAYMOND Oh Lord.

MERCY Now what am I sposeda do?

RAYMOND I don't know, do you have a safety pin?

MERCY A safety pin? Are you nuts? You think a safety pin is gonna hold up a pair of nylons? Give me a penny, you got a penny?

RAYMOND Yes, yes, I'm sure I have.

[*The school bell rings*]

MERCY Oh God, there's the bell. Hurry, wouldja hurry?
RAYMOND Yes, yes, I'm sure I saw a whole lot of pennies just ...
MERCY For Christ's sake I got a history test first period, Ray
come *onnn*
RAYMOND Ahah! Here we are, here –
[*she grabs it*]
Why this is miraculous, you can keep your stockings
up with a penny?
MERCY [*sobs*] Okay see ya
RAYMOND [*grabbing her*] Wait
MERCY I gotta –
RAYMOND Please, let me ... write you a note. I can write you a
note!
MERCY RAYMOND!
RAYMOND Please I – I've brought prophylactics – I thought today
–
MERCY PROPHYLACTICS! NO! No, no, no!! You're
disgusting! You're a disgusting old man and you
make me feel like a greasy slut and I hate you for it, I
haaaaate you, I hate you, I hate you, I ...
[RAYMOND *turns back into Italian man. The lights should
indicate that* MERCY *wakes up. Please don't use any hats or
anything to show the difference between* RAYMOND *and
the Italian; posture, etc. and lighting should be sufficient*]
MERCY [*turning away from him, mumbling*] Sorry – I thought
you were, I was having this dream, I thought you
were this guy I knew before –

Act One, Scene Five

MACK, DIERDRE's *husband, after having been asked to
leave by* DEE *about two weeks ago, has decided, in a
drunken moment, that he has to see her.* MACK *stumbles
through the courtyard quite drunk.*
TOILANE Hey, chief, gotta light?
MACK No, sorry man, don't smoke.
TOILANE Well throw you a fish.

MACK   Hey man, gimme a break. I'm just tryin to get home to my ...

TOILANE   NO, you give me a break, you give me a break and listen okay, just listen for once.

MACK   Hey, man, I don't know you, what're you

TOILANE   I just want to tell someone, okay? I just want to tell someone that I just seen the face of the woman that's gonna have my baby. She don't even know me, man but she is gonna have my baby cause ever since I first seen her, in a white skirt with long leather shoes, I felt something. GREEN get it? Like something GREEN like FLASH through our guts, together and I knew that I will spend my life, like inter-gutted with this lady, I KNEW MAN AND I KNOW that when we make love and I don't use the word lightly, it's gonna be like MAJOR WEATHER, LIKE MAJOR WEATHER, I think you know what I mean like MAJOR VIOLENT WEATHER [*very focused on* MACK]

MACK   ... Oh

TOILANE   And even tho she don't think I'm SHIT ON HER SHOE NOW I'm gonna git her!

MACK   Well! You got your work cut out for ya man. Good night!

TOILANE   I'm gonna get her and I'm gonna hold her till she's nothing but a warm puddle under my feet.

MACK   Good. Well, nice talking to you.

TOILANE   Thanks for the ear, man.

MACK   RIGHT!

TOILANE   You're alright.

Act One, Scene Six

DEE *is fingerpainting a large black blob, in a frenzied attempt to depict the 'animal' behind the wall that she so fears – on a large canvas.* MACK *puts his key in the lock, opens the door.*

DEE   MACK! What ... are you doing here?

MACK Did I wake you? I didn't wake you up did I?
[DEE *is silent*]
I saw the light on, I was passing by and I saw the light
on ... I just wanted to get those – books – I called you
about.
DEE At three o'clock in the morning?
MACK Your light was on.
DEE Okay, get the books.
MACK What are you doing up anyway? Painting?
DEE Yeah.
MACK So how are you?
DEE Fine.
MACK Your ... ah ... your family ... okay?
DEE Yuh, yes, my aunts are fine and my uncle's fine and
my sister's ... unstable as ever. How are yours?
MACK Fine. My brother and his wife just had a kid.
DEE Right. How'd it go.
MACK Good, good.
DEE Mack. This is all very nice but I really don't feel like
chatting right now, maybe we could have lunch or
something.
MACK Don't ever fucking do that to me. [*he points his finger
harder and harder at her*]
DEE Get your finger out of my face.
MACK DON'T EVER DO THAT TO ME.
DEE IF YOU DON'T GET YOUR FINGER OUT OF MY
FACE I'LL FUCKING KILL YOU, I'LL KILL YOU,
YOU UNDERSTAND?
MACK YOU WANT TO KILL ME? You want to kill me?
Okay. OK. Okay. Kill me, come on. Come on, kill me,
come onnnnn.
DEE Get out of here.
MACK NOOO you want to kill me, you kill me, kill me [*he
grabs her fist and rams the knuckle into his temple over and
over*] kill me, kill me kill me, kill me kill me kill me....
DEE [*starts to cry*] STOP IT, STOP IT, STOP IT,
MAAAAAACKIE.
MACK [*he stops, walks away, after a pause*] I don't ... get it. I
don't ... get ... why our marriage broke up. I lie awake
all night, all night sometimes I've got a burning hole,

and I think, I think and I think, what did I do, what
did I do, you never told me what I did?

DEE Nothing, you didn't do anything.

MACK It's not good enough, Dee, you wreck my life, you
have to tell me why. WHY DO YOU WANT US
APART?

DEE – I fell out of love. That happens. I'm sorry. I just fell
out of love.

MACK I don't believe you.

DEE I'm sorry.

MACK I don't believe you because of your eyes. Your eyes
have gone dead. Something's happened to you and
it's something to do with those nightmares you were
having –

DEE I don't have nightmares, the nightmares mean
nothing, I don't have night...

MACK DEE, you'd wake up and scream for five minutes, five
minutes, I'd hold you for five minutes while you ...
saw some unbelievable thing. [*pointing to blob*] What's
that, eh, eh what's that? Come on Dee, I know so much
about you. Your mother, your mother. Remember the
first time I went up to meet your mother; you were
going on about how scared you'd been on the
highway, how you would never drive on the highway
again and your mother in front of all of us, your
mother turned to you and said, 'Why? Why do YOU
want to live so much?' Remember what you did?
Remember what you did?

DEE Don't.

MACK Remember how you shook, you shook in the sleeping
bag with me all night you shook with your head in my
arms?

DEE No.

MACK I KNOW YOU.

DEE No.

MACK [*holds her*] You need me.
[*Long pause*]

DEE I don't love you. I don't –

MACK Nothing? Is ... there's nothing?

DEE Nothing. Nothing. I'm sorry.

MACK Okay. I don't believe you, but I guess ... if that's what you say, I believe you.... [*throws her the key*]
[MACK *walks off. After a moment* DEE *screams*]

DEE MAAAAAAAAAACKIE!!! MAAAAAAAAAACKIE!! [*she runs after him*] Come back, you've got to come back, I'm sorry, I'm sorry, I don't know what, it's like a devil possessed me, I didn't mean any of it, I do love you, I've always loved you, I lied, I don't know why, I'm sorry.

MACK GET AWAY FROM ME

DEE [*hanging on to his ankles*] Pleeeeease.

MACK Get ... away ... from ... me.

DEE Mackie!

MACK [*a cry from the heart*] GET AWAY!!

DEE [*crying*] You're the only person I ever loved, don't believe me, don't believe me when I say those things I was just cutting my own face, really, I love you, I ... please? ... please? Mackie, I am asking you with my whole being, please .... stay?

MACK I want you to promise me.
[*We can see* TOILANE *watching them*]

DEE Yes.

MACK Never, ever, ever ... again, okay?

DEE Never, ever, ever again.

MACK Once more, and I'm gone, I mean it, forever.

DEE Okay ... I promise.

MACK Boy ... boy.

DEE Oh God, I'm sorry, I'm sorry.

MACK I know, I know you are.
[DEE *smiles. They are facing each other. After quite a silence they go to kiss very tenderly, but just as their lips meet,* DEE *speaks*]

DEE Youuuuu sucker, you believe me? I HATE you, I still hate you, I just was scared to be alone, don't you get it, I'm using you I'M USING YOU, YOU WIMP. [*she starts to hit him across the face*] You suck, you suck, you suck, you suck, get out, get out, get out. [*she pushes him physically*] Get out! Go!!

MACK I'm warning you.

DEE I said get out of my life, and I mean it, don't believe the mewling pisshead, in the hall, believe me, I hate you, I hate you, I hate you!!!
[MACK *leaves*]
No, stay! Please stay, please stay! Go! Get out, get out! Stay! Go! [*she puts her head back and wails*]
MAAAAACKIEEEEE MACKKKKKIEEEEE MAAACKIEE.
[*As* DEE *wails 'MAAACKIE' we hear a siren, louder and louder. She collapses onto the floor*]
MAACKKKKIE what's happening to me?
MAAACKIE MAACKIE MACKIE.

Act One, Scene Seven

The siren stops. TOILANE *is in his watching position. His mother,* PEGGY CREESE, *a large, uneducated woman of great power, walks in.* TOILANE *is a bundle of nerves, after having watched the object of his love go through such a scene. Throughout the scene,* PEGS *cleans up the messy room.*

PEGS You gotta do something about those socks, Toi, all the men in this family have bad feet. YOUR FATHER'S socks coulda killed somebody on a bad day. I'm serious, like someone who was infirm or in their eighties.
TOILANE What are you doing here?
PEGS I'm talkin about your socks.
TOILANE Maa.
PEGS Shoppin' bozo, whatja think. Don't look like that, I told ya last night I said I'll come by six or seven-thirty, we'll go for a bite, and then, we'll start our Christmas shopping! ... Well it's the third Sarrday in October for buggy's sake, if ya don't start now you'll never get it done.
TOILANE I don't have no money.
PEGS Well why not?

TOILANE I ain't got paid yet.

PEGS Well that's a fine bed a petunias how're we supposed to go shoppin?

TOILANE I don't know.

PEGS Course if you lived home you wouldn't have to worry about money.

TOILANE If I lived home I'd be a retard.

PEGS Why do you say that.

TOILANE Cause anyone who's twenty-eight and still hasn't moved outa home is a retard.

PEGS You're outa your gourd. Anunciata next door, the Italian, all four of her sons are still at home and they're in their thirties and forties!

TOILANE Right, and look at em.

PEGS They're fine boys, that Dominic –

TOILANE They're retards, mum, the fat one with the small head? I seen him just standing up on the corner, just standing there at night, for hours, the other one, he's got them cataracts, don't even know he's sposda get an operation and the other one's a fag, is that what you want me to be, eh? A fag living with mummy?

PEGS Oh stop.

TOILANE You'd just like that wouldn't you?

PEGS What, if you was a queerbaby?

TOILANE Yeah, that'd make you happier than a pig in shit.

PEGS I got nothing against queerbabies, they're good for a laugh.

TOILANE Or a kick in the teeth.

PEGS You never.

TOILANE No.

PEGS Did you?

TOILANE Once in a while.

PEGS Oh that's cute, ya kill any? Eh? EH? I'M ASKIN YOU TOILANE, DID YOU KILL ANY?

TOILANE NO! I don't know, I don't know he just kept, like we'd kick his head and he'd move again so we'd kick it again and he wouldn't stop moving and I started seein like a monster from the cartoons with all these snake heads and everytime ya kick one off, it grows another one, right? And he kept growin snake heads so I kept

kickin them kickin them off and he goes 'I think I'm
swallowing blood' in this voice ... like Gramma or
something but he's a *guy*, he's a guy, right, he's not
GRAMMA, he's makin like he's Gramma and he's a
GUY.

PEGS   It's the bad fairy.

TOILANE What are you talkin about?

PEGS   At your christening, Freida Wilkinson, she hated my
guts cause she'd been going with your Dad for five
years when I come along, she put a curse on you.

TOILANE What are you talkin about?

PEGS   Just like in the story, the priest pours the water over
ya, you wailin your head off, and everybody comes up
to give good wishes, eh, well I turn around and there's
Freida Wilkinson, starin me eye to eye and she goes
'PEGGY CREESE THAT BABY IS IN FOR TROUBLE.'
I laughed eh, cause I thought she meant your howlin
but later that night I got the shakes just thinkin about
it, I was so cold nothing could get me warm not fifteen
blankets, nothin. She put a curse on you, and you lived
it out.

TOILANE What bullshit.

PEGS   Did you kill the man?

TOILANE WHY DIDN'T YOU HAVE MORE KIDS?

PEGS   You know damn well why I didn't have more kids,
what the heck are you talkin about.

TOILANE So ya stop buggin *me*, why didn't you have more kids?

PEGS   Because, BECAUSE, BECAUSE MY SISTER'S CHILD
Charlene, if you remember, weighed in at twenty-two
pounds at six years of age, SIX YEARS and today that
woman owns one-quarter of a pancreas, one kidney
and no spleen at all! She HATES my sister for bringin
her into this world, she HATES HER.
MY BROTHER HAS EPILEPSY THAT'S GOT SO
BAD HE HAS TO WALK AROUND WITH A
HOCKEY HELMET ON. I was not about to take the
chance of givin birth to another family catastrophe
and wear that bell around my neck all my life. NO
WAY NO WAY JOSE. NOW ASK ME AGAIN WHY I
didn't have any more kids.

TOILANE Okay, okay, okay, okay.

PEGS ASK ME AGAIN WHY I didn't have no more kids.

TOILANE Okay why didn't yas.

PEGS Cause you're the only one I want. [*pause*] You come home, ya'd have all your meals cooked, your shirts washed, ironed, you could come in as late as ya liked.

TOILANE Maa.

PEGS I wouldn't wait up for you. Heck, I'm conked out by half past eight!

TOILANE Ma.

PEGS It's easier for me this way, hell I'm livin the life of Riley, sleepin in till half past nine, havin frozen pies for dinner and a bag of timbits, nobody to worry about but my own sweet self. But think about it. If you had all that stuff taken care of and ya didn't have to worry about nothin you'd have time, time to think, to look in the paper for good jobs, to go back to school, to get trained. Trained to do something you're good at! Something you LIKE.

TOILANE STOP BUGGIN ME!! JUST STOP BUGGIN ME OKAY. THAT'S WHY I MOVED OUT CAUSE YA KEEP BUGGIN ME BUGGIN ME BUGGIN ME [*hits something*] FUCK.

[PEGS *goes to leave, very hurt*]

Maa.

[PEGS *stops with her back to him*]

How's your ... blood ... pressure....

PEGS High to bursting, in fact I think I feel a bloody nose comin on right now, yup, here it comes. [*lies down, gets out a kleenex*] See? Oh yah, I go to the doctor after Thanksgiving, he puts me on the scale, I've gained ten pounds, he goes, 'Whatja do, eat the whole turkey?' Now I did not eat a lot of that bird. Just a wing, a bit of white meat. Just a bit of soup and a sandwich now and then. I never touch the pies and pastries.

TOILANE Nope.

PEGS And he has to go and be so rude.

TOILANE Bastard.

PEGS And then, and then, I walk out the door and I see Ginny Richardson down the street, about a hundred

yards and that makes me feel sorta better, I mean, I
thought we'd have a little chat ... then she goes and
sees me and she's across the street in two seconds. She
crossed the street to avoid me, get it? She was trying
to avoid me, Toilane. Now why would she go and do
a thing like that?

TOILANE Cause ya talk too much.

PEGS How dare you.

TOILANE Well it's true, no one else is gonna tell you Mum, ya
got the talk trots.

PEGS Don't you be low.

TOILANE It's true.

PEGS It is not true. It is in no way true, and if it is, if it is, I
don't care. Because I happen to love the sound of my
voice. I think it's very nice and I happen to live alone
and I happen to need to talk to talk and talk and talk
and talk and don't nobody say nothing because I am
talking and I am gonna talk and talk till our feet freeze
off and our hands get frost bite cause when I am talkin
I am swimmin in a *big vat* of English cream – cream –
and talk and I want to swim and cream and talk and
talk till we all fall over and freeze.

TOILANE Jesus. You running a fever? Mum? What are you
talkin about everybody freezin?

PEGS Because we'd be standin outside, outside the
Dominion, that's where you run into people, that's
where they run away!

Act One, Scene Eight

TOILANE *makes his way up to* DEE's *apartment. She is
lying on the floor. He knocks again and again.*

DEE Yeah yeah yeah. [*she goes to the door*] Yes?

TOILANE Uh – superintendent?

DEE Oh. Yes?

TOILANE I'd like to talk to you for a minute, if ya don't mind.
Please. [TOILANE *is silent*]

DEE Is there a problem with the water? [*she leads him into the apartment*] I've noticed when I turn it on, it starts out dark brown. Come here, look at this. Have other people ... [*She looks at him. He is looking in an odd direction*] Is something wrong?

TOILANE No, no, it's not, no.

DEE Are you okay? Are you feeling okay?

TOILANE I'm – I have to tell you.

DEE What.

TOILANE Like, it's just that I like ... I ... I've seen you.

DEE Is this some kind of joke?

TOILANE I been watchin you, and – I – got this – I don't know.

DEE What do you mean?

TOILANE I mean ... I mean ... I mean that I would lie down on a bed of white hot coals for you to walk over, right on my back. I would fight four black guys, I'd go to the joint and do sixteen years I mean, I'd lose an eye, a leg ... I mean I want like, I want ... to be ... your knight ... like. I'm sweatin! I never said this to nobody before.

DEE A knight?

TOILANE A knight, like in the stories except now, modern, now, I'd give ya twenty-four-hour guard if you're nervous of burglars or rapists, I'll, I'll fuckin kill anybody that even ... even if they just say somethin that bugs ya, I'll kill em.

DEE You want to do all this ... for me? Me?

TOILANE I want to be your knight – with no armour.

DEE Why?

TOILANE Because – somepin' ... you got ... somepin ... like ME, somepin YOU know, you KNOW

DEE NO, no, I don't, I don't

TOILANE Yes, you do, Dee, I SEEN IT, ohhh you do!

DEE NO.

TOILANE Let her go, Dee, come on, come on, NOW

DEE ... [*whisper*] But I'm sooo scared ...

TOILANE It's okay, I gotcha, it's okay.

DEE It's ... okay?

TOILANE It's okay. It's okay. It's okay...
[*She turns her head in such a way to indicate that she is 'ready' to 'let her go'*]

Act One, Scene Nine

MERCY You do so remember, you do SO, you say you don't,
you're lying cause I was there, I was there and you
were there: twenty below, twenty below zero running
to catch the school bus, all my books fall in the snow, I
gotta pick them up, so I miss the bus, have to hitch.
Stick my thumb out, this guy pulls over, old English
guy in an old blue car, I get in, his name's Raymond,
Raymond Brisson, he gives me a smoke, we get
talking and like he's really intelligent, he's read *Lord of
the Rings*, THREE TIMES, and like, I'm thinking, this
guy could be my *boyfriend*!! Like none of the other
guys at school would even look at me, but this guy,
RAYMOND, he SEES, see? He sees what I always
knew ... that there's something ... like a STAR in me,
something, like if they REALLY knew me, even the ...
truly GREAT would love me ... cause I got –
something ...
   So we park at the school, bell goes off, 'Oh my God,
I gotta go,' he looks at me, goes, 'You know, you might
be quite pretty if you lost some of that poundage' ...
He said that. He actually ... believed me to be ... lovely.
Lovely.
   Not like you you FUCKER DADDY. I HEARD you,
I SAW you giving her that locket 'for my favourite
daughter, *Deirdre*' – that heart with the ICH BIN DEIN
engraved. What does that mean, anyway, eh? What
the hell does that mean?
   So he leans over, his eyes going yellow and he
kisses me, put his ... tongue right in my mouth ... like
an egg cracking open in my belly pouring out all this
like ... honey everywhere, GOD I wanted to kiss him
again and again. Shit the bell, 'I really gotta go, but
but, I think I'll hitchhike tomorrow' then I see *you
guys*, leaning up against the wall, having your smoke
before class, and I walk by you, almost past you, don't
want to be late, when

'YOU DROPPED SOMETHING'
I feel my face turning red; like Christ, what if
something dropped from my body or something but I
keep going anyway
'HEY WHOREDOG, WE SAID YOU DROPPED
SOMETHING'
Oh my NO, that word, no, my heart's falling through
my chest, SHIT, they saw they SAW your tongue in
my mouth, and my underpants, they know, they
know, they're all – SHIT I can't move, I can't move
cause I know I know that they KNOW that they
KNOW that I'm a 'HEY WHOREDOG! YA GONNA
DO FOR US WHAT YA DID FOR THAT OLD MAN?'
    I can't cry, NO please GOD don't let me, I shut my
eyes, waiting, just waiting for them to go in, I still can't
move, I'm just standing there why can't I move when
OWWWW! SOMETHING hit me in the EYE what the
OWW!! OWWW! STOP IT what ... WHAT – pennies!
They're throwing ... pennies at me I don't get it, like
what should I do? Nobody – told me – how to act how
come GOD, OWW please, how could anyone have so
much pennies, and why are they throwing them at me,
what did I OWW oh no, oh no this is so bad please,
Mummy ... when poof I know what to do, I know. So I
just bend over, I bend over and I ... pick up their
pennies one by one, all hot and greasy, I pick em up –
they're still hitting my back, till my fists ... are stuffed,
stuffed and I stand up and I walk right to em with my
fists out like this [*demonstrates*] right up to em and I go
I say, 'Here, here's your pennies back.' Then they're
gone, and I'm standing there ... so when I see you you
know, even though it's twenty years later, it's today,
you know? It's now like no time's passed, all now and
I still can't look at a penny, I can't, cause it makes me
know, you see, it makes me know that I ... am a sick,
disgusting whore for letting a guy's tongue in my
mouth and especially, especially for letting that ...
honey pour that ... feeling ... that I certainly never ...
ever ... had ... again.
[*The* OLD ITALIAN MAN *kisses her on the eyelids*]

Thank-you, you ... even though you no capiche Inglese, you capiche, eh? My girlfriend Virginia? She told me that you only know a guy loves you if he kisses you on the eyelids. Isn't that stupid? Hey, are you cold?

MAN Freddo, molto freddo.

MERCY Here, take my sweater.

Act One, Scene Ten

Bus station. MERCY, *just arriving in town, runs into* MACK, *who is just leaving.*

MERCY Maaack! Hi! How'd you know I was coming? How are ya?

MACK Fine, okay. Look, Mercy? I'm sorry, but ... I'm not here to pick you up.

MERCY Uh oh. Is something wrong between you and Dee?

MACK I'm just going to visit my brother for a couple of days.

MERCY Oh no. Oh gee – that's too bad. I was hoping you'd give me a job at your bookstore.

MACK Sure – maybe – later.

MERCY Oh. It sounds bad.

MACK Well, anyway, here's my bus.

MERCY Mack? Do you think it's for – it's not for good is it?

MACK I don't know Mercy.

MERCY Oh. Well, then can I tell you something? I just ... you know when we would cut green beans together at the Thanksgiving dinners of Mum's ... did you feel ... did you ever feel ... you know....
[MACK *smiles*]
Why don't you miss the bus. We'll go to the washroom, I'll give you a [*whispers 'blow job'*]

MACK Mercia, stop. You don't know what you're saying. I am your sister's husband.

MERCY You really love her, don't you.

MACK See you later.

MERCY Oh God, I'm so embarrassed, you must think I'm a slut, you must think I'm a slut.

MACK You didn't mean it.
[MACK *kisses her eyelids. She takes this to have meaning. It doesn't*]
Give my best to your sister.
MERCY Yah. Yah. [MERCY *touches her eyelids, rubs them hard*]

Act One, Scene Eleven

TOILANE *is sitting in* DEE's *living room, smoking.* DEE *comes out of the bedroom.*
TOILANE Hey, smoke?
[DEE *is silent*]
Hey, what's the matter?
DEE Just....
TOILANE You look nice with your hair messed up, pretty. Hey ... hey.
DEE Please.
TOILANE What's the matter?
DEE I – I want you to go.
TOILANE Deedree....
DEE Please, just....
TOILANE Are you feelin shamed? You shouldn't feel shamed, you were
DEE Please go
TOILANE You're beautiful. You're the most beautifullest woman I....
DEE Listen, I know that you're the superintendent here, but ... other than for those kinds of things, I never want to see you. Do you understand?
TOILANE But ... but ... what we just been through ... you ... you ... can't do that after what we just been through, how can you?
DEE It was nothing, you understand? NOTHING
TOILANE It was so Deedree.
DEE No!
TOILANE You showin me your ... your animal.
DEE NO!
TOILANE You shown me.

DEE   Please go, please

TOILANE   No, I won't go, I won't....

DEE   GOOOOO!! GOOO! GOOO! GOOO! Get out of here!
Get out of here!!

[TOILANE *goes to hug her, she pushes him away, she hits*
him, he stops her, she falls on the ground and bursts into
sobs]

TOILANE   Hey ... hey ... Jeez, you must be Catholic or somethin,
are you Catholic? I used to go out with this Catholic
girl, Linda, she'd cry after but ... you, you're acting
crazy.

DEE   Listen, you said that you would do anything for me. I
just ... want ... you to please

TOILANE   What?

DEE   Leave, I want –

TOILANE   I think you don't know what you want. I think from
what I seen in there, that I'm what you wanted all
your life.

[DEE *sobs*]

Okay, okay, okay. I won't talk about it, I won't talk
about it and I'll go if you want, but ... I'll be there, I'll
be right down there waitin for you when you come to
your senses ... and you know, when I was in high
school I broke off with a girl cause she reclined on the
first date, like lay down, in the car, but I changed now.
I still respect ya! I respect ya.

[*Knock, knock*]

DEE   [*to him*] Who's that?

[TOILANE *shrugs*]

Who is it?

MERCY   ME!

DEE   Who is me?

MERCY   Me, for God's sake, open the door!

DEE   I'm coming, I'm coming. [*opens door*] ... Yes?

MERCY   Dee, it's me!

DEE   I'm sorry, I don't....

MERCY   You don't *recognize* me?

DEE   I'm sorry – were you at Joan's the other night, or

MERCY   JOAN'S? Dee, it's me, your sister, Mercy, Jesus,
what's wrong with you?

DEE Merc! Merc! Oh God, God, I'm sorry, I'm sorry. I ... guess ... I've just been kind of upset – about –

MERCY Mack.

DEE [*looks at her for a second, wondering how she knows about Mack*] Merc, this is Toilane Creese, Toi, this is Mercia, my sister. I haven't seen her in a year and, and ...

TOILANE Nice to meet you.

MERCY Toilane, I've never heard that name before, is that ... foreign?

TOILANE No, not really, my mum named me after our Chinese landlady's son ... Toi ... she was really good friends with our landlady, like we used to go to their Chinese New Year's and that, so, you know ... it's kinda weird, I know....

MERCY I think it's nice.

[*Pause*]

DEE WELL, Toi, I'm sure I'll see you around the building ... Toilane is the superintendent.

TOILANE Good at fixin things ... handy.

MERCY Oh!

TOILANE Well, I guess I'd better be goin ... leave you two long-lost sisters to ... um ... talk ... or whatever. [*to* DEE] I'll maybe see you around?

DEE I'll call you if I need anything fixed.

[TOILANE *goes to kiss* DEE, *she avoids him.* TOILANE *exits*]

MERCY WHAT was THAT?

DEE How did you know about Mack?

MERCY Why didn't you recognize me, DEEDEE, your own sister?

DEE I said how did you know about Mack? Answer me please.

MERCY NO YOU TELL ME WHY YOU DIDN'T RECOGNIZE ME?!

DEE Because ... I don't know, you're not supposed to be here, you're supposed to be three thousand miles away ... what are you doing here?

MERCY I came to visit.

DEE How did you know about Mack?

MERCY I'M YOUR SISTER WHY DIDN'T YOU RECOGNIZE
YOUR OWN SISTER?

DEE What do you want me to do, go down on my knees
and bang my head against the floor? I'm sorry, okay?
I'm sorry, I'm sorry, I'm sorry. [*she falls to her knees*]

MERCY [*crying a little*] It just makes me feel you don't want me
here.

DEE Oh come on, I'm just shocked! You just show up after
a year – I haven't even heard from you in three
months.

MERCY You don't! You don't want me here!

DEE Whether or not I want you here is beside the point. I
want to know why you have come. Where's Tony?
What happened? Did something happen?

MERCY Do you want to know where I saw Mackie?
[DEE *looks*]
The bus station.

DEE His brother.

MERCY Yeah, he said something about that.

DEE How did he seem?

MERCY Sad.
[DEE *nods*]
Is it permanent?

DEE So what happened with Tony? Are you ...

MERCY He came home Wednesday night and said, 'I'm
moving in with Gina' ... She's the slut who works in
the store.

DEE You had no ... inkling?

MERCY No. I mean when I think of it now there were lots of
things; the fact that we, we'd go out to a restaurant
and go through a whole meal without saying a word.

DEE Why?

MERCY What would we say? If I said 'Hey look at that lady
over there she looks so lonely' he'd say 'What are you
talking about' so all we'd ever talk about was the
food.

He had this thing, you know? Where we could only
have sex once a week, every Sunday, between the
news and the late movie? And once, I think it was

Wednesday or Thursday, after work, I had these white pantyhose on and I was feeling, you know, horny? So he was lying there on the bed watching TV, holding that converter, pushing around the channels, and I you know, climbed on top of him, and ... sort of whispered to him that if he felt like fooling around, well he threw me right off him and starts yelling 'It's Thursday, it's Thursday you cow, not Sunday, so don't pressure me, don't pressure me, don't ever pressure me again!' So I start crying, you know, just softly and I guess he felt sorry for me, so he says, 'Listen, if you can get it up, you can have it, but I'm watching *The Brady Bunch*.' So *The Brady Bunch* came on and I ... rode ... him, I took off my panty hose and underpants and I rode him, here I am moaning and groaning while he's chuckling away at something on *The Brady Bunch*. Do you ... mind ... like ... if I stay here ...? For a while? Dee? What's wrong with you, are you alright? You're shaking like a....

DEE   I'm SO COLD. My body must be in some kind of shock, SHIT.

MERCY   Come here. Put your head on my lap. That's a girl, that's a girl. I was shaking when Tony left too, I swear it's perfectly natural after *ten* years of marriage! Of course you're in shock. Oh boy, it's a good thing I'm here to take care of you kid, you need a nurse!

DEE   Merc, Merc, you know that fear I used to have of an animal?

MERCY   Behind the wall?

DEE   Yeah, well it's like something's happened to me. It's like it got out of the wall. Like a shark banging at the shark cage and sliding out. Out of the wall and inside me. I feel something taking over. I don't....

MERCY   It's just Mack, really

DEE   No, no, you don't understand. I have these dreams, I have orgasms, I have orgasms in my sleep, I wake up with my nipples hard but the dream, the dream that carried it was so horrible, so horrible that....

MERCY   How horrible could it be, were you devouring Mummy's brains and spitting out her teeth....

DEE I'm afraid. I'm afraid that the dreams will seep into the day. That I'll do things – that I'll....

MERCY Is that why you broke up with Mack. Dee? Is it?

DEE I don't know. He's the only person I ever wanted. I don't –

MERCY Well, sounds to me like you did the right thing.

DEE I did?

MERCY Well yes. I mean, a man would bring this thing forth, wouldn't he? Or a baby. Dee, you mustn't have a baby.

DEE Why?

MERCY Who knows what might happen. Who knows what you could do. You could do horrible things. Mum knew that about you – Dee? Knife old ladies in the head. Screw old winos in the park. When people let their animal out they go to the top of tall buildings and shoot forty people.

DEE Oh God.

MERCY I know you Dee, I'm your sister. Mum knew you. I know what you could do. No, you don't want Mackie. I'm here now. I'll take care of you. I know you. Poor baby, you're really still a baby, aren't you.

DEE Sing that song, sing that song you used to sing when I was little and scared of the animal, sing that song.

MERCY Weee ... are ... walking ... togetherr ... in the nice weatherrr

Ohhh what a lovely dayyyy....

Weee ... are walking ... togetherrr ... in the nice weatherr....

ohhhh what a lot of fuuuunnn....

[DEE *joins in; after, she falls asleep*] You know when you have wild sex with a guy like that they stick to you like glue. I mean, I know you probably had to do something wild cause of Mackie, but how are you going to get rid of him?

[DEE *is asleep.* MERCY *smiles*]

We are ... walking ... together ... in the ni-ice ... weather, oh what a lovely....

Act One, Scene Twelve

MACK *comes out on ramp the same way* TOILANE *did, addressing the audience.*

MACK First just one, buzzing around, then two, three we barely notice, then wham! someone gets stung, something's going on – what, what is it? Call in the pest people, 'gotta be a nest' they say, 'behind the wall, a nest'! Shit! We call in the contractors, gotta do something, somebody could have an allergy, DIE; they knock down the wall, just BASH the thing down; all this dust, white dust, plaster, everywhere, and there standing there, six feet high, *there,* this ... honeycomb, dripping, drenched, pouring out ... honey into the store, this ... structure ... thousands of bees, *fifty thousand* BEES, living there all the time, serving the queen, all the time, while we, on the other side – doing cash, taking inventory – these bees were building, building, *making.* The pest people, they get this SPRAY, this green shit and they carve these HOLES in it
They CARVE
Her fear about things ... behind walls?
Her ... eyes?

Act One, Scene Thirteen

DEE *is on the phone to the pharmacist. We see her canvas, which she has painted with a black line inside a brilliant yellow circle. Only she and the canvas are lit.*

DEE Hi, I bought a pregnancy test from you this morning, and I seem to have lost the instructions ... could you tell me what a black line means? A black line inside a brilliant yellow circle?
[TOILANE *is watching her, from his glass door. He sits and smokes and watches*]

142

Act One, Scene Fourteen

Hospital. DEE, *having left her pre-surgery bed and wandered down the halls, in her gown, walks towards the audience as we hear the doctors paged. She has felt the life of the fetus inside her and cannot go through with the abortion. She now walks towards the audience – she addresses the audience as if it is the fetus.*

P.A. Calling Doctor Samuels, Doctor Samuels to Emerg, Doctor Samuels, calling Doctor Rank, Doctor Rank to the O.R., Doctor Rank, calling Doctor Johnson, Doctor Deborah Johnson to Maternity, Doctor Deborah Johnson, calling Doctor Roch, Doctor Roch please, calling Doctor Domovitch, Doctor Domovitch, calling Doctor French, Doctor French....

DEE Is that you? Are you ... speaking ... to me? I can hear you breathing, speaking. STOP, PLEASE! STOP SPEAKING TO ME NOOOO! I don't want to hear you STOP. STOP talking to me – you're breathing, in my ears, stop. Please, no! I DON'T want to KNOW you, NO, PLEASE, I WANT TO GET RID OF YOU I – don't. Don't. DON'T make those ... [*she sees something that touches her – such as a baby's smile, a small hand, etc.*] don't – no, no no no OKAY! OKAY OKAY OKAY YOU ARE! You are! You are!! YOU ARE!!!

Act One, Scene Fifteen

DEE, *still in her hospital gown, at home with* MERCY. *On her canvas is the grotesque painting of a ten-week-old fetus.*

DEE I could hear it, Mercy, I could see it, see it, sending these flashes these flashes of life.

MERCY You're telling me that you were lying on the bed, all ready to be wheeled into the operating room, the poor gynaecologist was putting on his scrubs and you took off? You just left?

143

DEE   You don't understand!

MERCY   You're not allowed to do that, Dee.

DEE   But I saw it! I SAW THE LIFE that I was about to have SUCKED, VACUUMED –

MERCY   Oh my GOD you haven't gone PRO-LIFE on me!

DEE   IT'S NOT OKAY. *It's not okay to take this life this life is LIVING.*

MERCY   BULLSHIT, DEE, BULLSHIT, I've been pregnant THREE times, THREE, and I've never felt a thing, the thing is like an INSECT.

DEE   Nooooo.

MERCY   You think I'm some kind of BUTCHER?

DEE   You're asleep, that's all, you don't know what you're doing, this ... child ... woke me up.

MERCY   Okay, well what are you going to do then, Pollyanna? What are you going to do? ... Could you suckle a baby with Toilane's face? Could you, Dee? Deedee? Aren't you afraid of what your ANIMAL might do? Look at the girl on the news last night who threw her baby into the lake, Dee, what are you going to do?

DEE   I don't know.

MERCY   Are you going to give it to him, to Toilane?

[DEE *stares at* MERCY]

You have to decide, Dee. You can't just not know. You have to decide. [MERCY *shakes her*] Deirdre!

DEE   Leave me alone! Leave me alone! Do you hear me? Leave me –

[TOILANE, *who has been listening at the door, opens it*]

TOILANE   It's funny, I sorta knew I madja pregnant. I pictured, you know? While we were doin it. I pictured in my mind, this face, lookin at me, this ... face.

DEE   Listening at people's doors is a criminal offence.

TOILANE   I want to marry you.

DEE   It was a one-night stand, Toi.

TOILANE   Don't be ashamed, please, don't be ashamed. I love you. I want to marry you, I want – our child together, I –

[*He offers a ring, she kicks it away*]

DEE   WILL YOU WAKE UP? I'm having this baby and I am giving it away. Get it? Get it?

TOILANE You're giving my baby away? You're givin my baby away?

DEE I'm giving your baby away, yes.
[*There is a long pause.* TOILANE *goes down to the courtyard to cry*]

MERCY THAT WAS A HIDEOUS thing to do.

DEE [*starts changing*] Fuck off.

MERCY That was a disgusting, cruel, horrific ...

DEE GET OFF MY CASE Mercia.

MERCY No, no this time I will not get off your case.

DEE Oh cut the sabre-toothed tiger routine, really.

MERCY You make me sick you are so smug and beautiful, you have no idea what it is to be me, all the boys looking straight at you, never at me. That time at the dance when you went right up to Stephen Gilroy who you knew was crazy about you and said 'Oh dance with Mercy, she loves you so much.' And the other time in front of all our friends when you made me pick my nose and eat it; you said I had to, to get in your club that you'd all done it. And then I did it. And you laughed, you laughed. Do you know how much I hated you? Do you know how much?

DEE Oh come on Mercia.

MERCY If you're – a woman and you're – born ugly you might as well be born dead.
[DEE *giggles*]
Don't! Don't you laugh!

DEE Really, Merc, I think you've been watching too much television.

MERCY Don't put down television. DON'T YOU FUCKING PUT DOWN TELEVISION, YOU SNOT, TELEVISION HAS SAVED MY LIFE. IT HAS LITERALLY SAVED MY LIFE, WHEN YOU'RE SO LONELY YOU COULD DIE. I MEAN SHRIVEL UP AND DIE BECAUSE NOBODY CARES WHETHER YOU GET UP OR STAY IN BED OR DON'T EAT, WHEN YOU'RE SO LONELY EVERY PORE IN YOUR SKIN IS SCREAMING TO BE TOUCHED, THE TELEVISION IS A SAVIOUR. IT IS A VOICE A WARM VOICE. THERE ARE FUNNY TALK SHOWS

WITH HOSTS WHO THINK EXACTLY LIKE I DO.
And when the silence in your apartment, the silence is
like a big nothing and you're thinking, my God, my
God, is this what life is? Years and years and years of
this? You turn on the television and you forget about
it. Often all I'll think about all day at work is what's on
TV that night, especially in the fall, with the new
shows, I get really, genuinely excited. I ... I love
television. I love it. It makes me happy so don't put it
down. [*she exits*]

Act One, Scene Sixteen

MACK *goes through the courtyard. He sees* TOILANE
sobbing against the wall. MACK *stops, looks at* TOILANE.

MACK I hope whatever it is ... passes.
[MACK *knocks on* DEE's *door. The grotesque painting of a
three-month fetus is replaced by a beautiful one of a four-
month fetus*]

DEE Hi. Come in. Can I get you some tea?

MACK Sure. Okay.

DEE It looks like quite the storm out there.

MACK Biggest one of the season they say.

DEE Yah?

MACK Yeah.

DEE So, how have you been?

MACK Oh, oh, you know; okay. Look, Dee is this just a visit
or –

DEE I wanted to see you. I've missed you so – I feel it all
here. [*puts her hand on her chest*] It's like this great
weight here. Do you ever....

MACK DON'T.

DEE I try not to think about you but then I dream about
you every night. Last night you were holding my –
skull in fragments – like a teacup and you held it
together – in your hands – you –

MACK DEE, forget it.

DEE I know I have no right at all after my terrible
behaviour but – every footstep on the stair, Mack,
your voice....

MACK DON'T PLAY WITH ME, PLEASE DON'T.

DEE I'm serious, Mack.

MACK Yeah, just like my two-year-old nephew says, 'I want
juice' and then you give it to him and he throws it on
the floor.

DEE NO. NO not like your two-year-old nephew, I'm
serious. Look, what I said before, that night, it was like
an illness. An infection or something. Encephalitis. I
don't know. Whatever it is it's gone. It's gone and it'll
never happen again. I wanted to call you for a while
now, but I was scared, afraid, really. I've been
watching out the window every day in case you –
[MACK *gets up to go*]
Mack, I want you to come back.

MACK How can I know if you're serious?

DEE Well for one thing, I'm pregnant.

MACK So, what, you want me to hold your hand on the way
to the clinic, be there when you come out of the
anaesthetic?

DEE I'm keeping this one. I'm already three and a half
months. Mack, it – spoke to me – I literally got up off
the stretcher and walked out of the *hospital*. Mack –
Mack?

MACK You walked out of the hospital?

Act One, Scene Seventeen

PEGS *sees* TOILANE *sobbing on the ground in the
courtyard. She approaches him.*

PEGS I don't know if you lost your job or some girl give ya
your walking papers, but whatever it is, I don't think
you'd want your father to see you take it lying down.
Get up Toi. Get up off the ground.

Act One, Scene Eighteen

MACK *and* MERCY *are chopping green peppers, hard on large wooden block. First we hear the chopping sound.* MERCY *is aroused. We see* MACK *become aware of this and move away.*

MERCY So uh, I hate to be like nosy, but, like are you guys back together? You spend an awful lot of time in the bedroom.

MACK How small do you want these things anyway?

MERCY Oh Mack, stop being such a GUY, are you together or not?

MACK Yes.

MERCY What happened?

MACK You are a sticky beak. [*he puts a vegetable on her nose*]

MERCY I just think it's ridiculous.

MACK Awwww.

MERCY Well she doesn't love you.

MACK Hey, hey, easy.

MERCY Well she doesn't. I might as well tell you the truth. She's told me.

MACK [*sings*] Here we go a chopping greens, chopping greens, chopping greens....

MERCY Are you staying because of the baby?

MACK You shut your mouth and keep chopping.

MERCY But you're happy about the baby?
[MACK *smiles*]
Why her? Why her Mack? What ... does she have?

MACK Come on, Merc, don't....

MERCY I just want to know, after she treats you like absolute SHIT on her SHOE, what is it you see in her?

MACK She doesn't have your nice big bum, that's for sure.

MERCY DON'T PATRONIZE ME. I WANT TO KNOW WHAT YOU SEE IN HER.

MACK I'm sorry, what can I say?

MERCY [*approaching him*] Do you find me at all attractive?

MACK Yes, of course, you're very attractive.

MERCY Would you ... kiss me?

MACK Merc....

MERCY Please? Nobody's kissed me in so long. My husband never kissed me not for years, we'd just do it in the dark facing separate directions. Please?

[MACK *walks towards her, kisses her, a nice, long kiss, she wants more, he backs off, pats her on the back in a friendly way*]

Oh the weight, the weight of a man, you know? I miss that ... weight. Hey you've got lipstick on your face, really!

[DEE *puts her key in the door, comes in*]

DEE I just had the most amazing cab driver! He'd been driving for forty-two years, FORTY-TWO, he was three years in the marines and then he got his hack license, he told me he said, 'I hate this city, I hate the other cabbies, I hate the road and most of all, most of all,' he says, 'I hate the riding public!' Don't you love that, 'the riding public'? – Where're you going?

MACK Shit! I have to be at the store in ... four minutes ago.

DEE Aren't you eating dinner with us?

MACK Yeah, yeah, yeah, this is just a meeting, I have a meeting, it's one-third my store, I should be there.

DEE [*kisses him*] Okay. See you soon!

MACK Bye Merc. [*he leaves*]

DEE [*still laughing, putting down bags*] 'The riding public,' I LOVE THAT.

MERCY HOW COULD YOU DO THAT?

DEE What?

MERCY Tell him that it's HIS baby, don't you think he'll be suspicious when the kid doesn't look ANYTHING like him.

DEE I told you, I'm giving it away, the Children's Aid has the *perfect* couple.

MERCY Does he know that?

DEE No.

MERCY Well when are you going to tell him, you have to tell him!

DEE When I'm sure I have my roots in him.

MERCY What about your animal or whatever it was. Aren't you TERRIFIED you might –

DEE   Oh that, that was just – I was under a huge amount of pressure at work, it....

MERCY   BULLSHIT, it's not gone, it's taken over you. It is you. You're body-snatched. That's why you're behaving so atrociously.

DEE   How am I behaving?

MERCY   USING MACK, USING....

DEE   FUCK OFF DO YOU HEAR ME? I DON'T WANT TO HEAR ANOTHER FUCKING WORD ABOUT MACK. I DON'T WANT TO HEAR....

[MERCY *begins to freak out, she rips newspaper in* DEE's *face and screams*]

MERCY   I want ... to be the centre, I want to be the centre of somebody's life. I haven't been the centre since Mum died, she made me the centre, she sat up when I came in she asked me what I got at the store and how was the bank today and didn't think I was overqualified for my work. She said I looked tired and it was too cold for me out there and nobody does that! NOBODY!

You know, I'm so ... stupid, so loathsome that I actually, I had this friend in Vancouver, that was dying of a brain tumour? And I wished on my birthday, I wished that I would get one so that I could have that kind of kindness ... from people. [*pause*] How can anybody like me, eh? How can you like me? I mean would you like me if I wasn't your sister? Would you?

DEE   You were very kind to me when I was little. You're a very ... kind person.

Act One, Scene Nineteen

PEGS *and* TAXI DRIVER.

PEGS   Your children are only loaned to you, that's what Muriel said; they're only loaned to you for a short time.... It comes as quite a shock to us, you know, us girls who been brought up to think family is our

whole life and ya grow up and ya get married and ya
start havin kids and you are in your prime, man,
everybody on the street smiles, they respect ya, you're
the most powerful thing there is, a mother, with
young kids, and the kids think you're Christmas, they
want to sit on your knee, and help ya bake cookies,
Mum this, Mum that, and you're tired as hell but
you're having the time of your LIFE, right? You're
important, you're an important member of society,
kids all around you, friend's kids, sister's kids, car
pools, Round Robin – you're havin a ball! And then
they get older, ya go back to work, and it's their
friends, their friends are more important than you,
than anything in the world, ya couldn't drag them out
on a picnic for a million dollars, and it seems they only
talk to you if it's to get money or the car. They whip
through their meals in about ten seconds flat,
something took you five hours of buying and
chopping and mixing and cooking and then they leave
the house. And ya never see em, and ya wonder if
they hate you. You know they're only there because of
the money thing, they'd be gone in a second if there
was a chance. Why is that? Why don't they like you
anymore? I tried; you know, I tried like hell to listen to
the AC-DC and the Led Zepplin and all that, even said
I liked it, I did like that 'Stairway to Heaven' one, I
used to get jokes from the magazines, newspapers,
you know, a Mum with a sense of humour? That went
over like a lead balloon. I'd drive him to his parties,
his roller skatin, his hockey and baseball, we'd go the
whole drive silent, not a single word. Only word was
at the end, 'Pick me up at eight o'clock.' ... What
happened? What happened to the baby who looked
up at me with eyes when the doctor first showed him
to me, blackberry eyes, the baby I musta walked ten
miles a day in our little apartment, back and forth,
back and forth, eyes closin, lookin at me, lookin at me.
Why is it that look goes away?

DRIVER Three seventy-five, please, lady?

PEGS I know. I know how much it is.

Act One, Scene Twenty

MERCY, MACK *and* DEE *are all sitting around having after-dinner drinks.*

MACK So, Dad DIES at the top of the stairs, massive heart attack right on the top stair well LUCY, our DOG was at the bottom, she goes berserk, howling like a banshee, wouldn't let a soul near him, they had to shoot her with a stun gun; two days later she has a stroke, you'd go into the house, it's pitch dark and there was my mother passed out on the couch with a bottle of Scotch and this DOG with a paralyzed bark.

[MACK *renders a dog's paralyzed bark*]

DEE She's a sweet dog, golden Labrador.

MERCY Uh oh, I can feel my boils starting.

DEE What do you mean?

MERCY EVERY time I drink red wine I get boils, it's incredible, these huge red things and if I try and squeeze them they just go to twice the size, it's a curse.

MACK Well when you hear what they put in wine these days.

DEE Anti-freeze.

MACK WHAT?

DEE Whatever the scientific word for anti-freeze is, that's what they put in, I think.

MACK So, Mercy, you haven't said a word about your new job. Are you bored to death?

MERCY Apparel can be really interesting you know. I used to work lingerie? And I got so I could tell a girl's size as soon as she walked through the door, winter coat and everything, she'd come in right? and she'd say, 'I'd like a 36B please,' and I'd go, 'I'm sorry but you're not gonna need anything bigger than an "A,"' and she'd get all huffy with me but then she'd try it on and I'd be right! She'd go, 'How'd you know?' and I'd go, 'I don't know, I just know!' I just knew!

MACK But ... how?

MERCY Ohh it's a talent, I guess, a creative talent.

MACK Come on, you're trying to tell me you could guess somebody's bra size under a winter coat?

MERCY Yes Mack, why, do you think I'm lying? Do you think I would lie about it?

DEE He's not suggesting you're lying Merc, we're just wondering how you could determine a woman's bra size if she's wearing a coat.

MERCY ... From her face to tell you the truth. Girls of different bra sizes wear different faces, like, if you're a 28, right, you've been that all your life, so you have a certain ... you're all looking at me thinking I'm incredibly stupid.

MACK I know what you mean. I ... have the same talent with suit size.

MERCY ... Suitcase!

DEE What?

MERCY The word suitcase means suit ... case, like case for suits, did you ever think of that? I mean it's amazing, I just never ... thought of it....
[*Knock, knock, knock at the door; repeats*]

MACK [*joking*] Go away! Go away!

MERCY I'll get it.

MACK No, I'll get it.

MERCY No, I'll get it.

MACK No I'll get it.

MERCY No I'll get it.

MACK Okay, you get it.
[MERCY *gets it. It is* PEGS *and* TOILANE. PEGS *pushes* MERCY *out of the way*]

PEGS [*now addressing the room*] THE HECK WITH THIS. THE HECK WITH THIS. [*snaps her fingers*] TOI! Come on, we're gonna have a talk with these people.

DEE Pardon me, I don't believe....

PEGS Asked or not, we're comin honey and you're sitting down and you're gonna listen up. Sit down.

DEE No. I don't have to sit down, what are you....

PEGS You know damn well why I'm here now sit down.

MACK Sit down Dee, the lady has something to say. Spice things up a little.

DEE Mack, I....

MACK Come on! We'll all sit down!

DEE If you don't leave I'm calling the police.

MACK Oh my God there's no need to bring the police into this my dear, let's listen to what the woman has to say.

DEE Well, I'm leaving then, you can all stay here.

MACK Dee, come on, relax.

PEGS Enough of this stupidity. YOU are gonna give my grandchild away over my DEAD BODY. [*terrible pause*] You hear me?

DEE I'm sorry, I really don't know what you're talking about.

PEGS You know damn well what I'm talking about slut, and you're not gettin away with it. I got the best lawyer in this city workin on the case and we are gonna win hands down. And not only are we gonna get our baby, but you are gonna pay us for damages through the TEETH, understand?

DEE I'm sorry, I really think you have the wrong apartment.

MACK What is this?

PEGS You the husband are ya? How's it feel to be married to a two-timin' slut who gives babies away?

MACK Look, I'm sure this has all arisen from a misunderstanding, surely we can....

PEGS There's no misunderstandin here. Your wife had sexshul relations with my son ... on this floor ... and made him do funny things. After I spent twenty-three years teaching him to respect a woman. And then she told me herself that she was pregnant with his kid, and that she was gonna give it away. Cause she didn't want her baby with people like us. Am I right?

DEE Look, Mrs....

PEGS Creese, Margaret Creese.

DEE Mrs. Creese, your son, came up one day to borrow some milk, or that was the excuse he made, and then he proceeded to assault me; he ripped my blouse and held a knife to my throat and I don't know what else he would have done had my sister not come in.

MACK What is going on? Did this guy try to....

DEE   It's okay Mack.

TOILANE [*pointing to* MERCY] YOU KNOW! YOU KNOW
CAUSE YOU HEARD HER TELL ME THAT IT WAS
MINE. YOU WERE HERE. TELL THEM, TELL
THEM WHAT YA HEARD.

DEE   My sister would be only too happy to tell you what
she heard, we have nothing to hide.

MERCY Would you excuse me please? [*she leaves*]

PEGS   I don't know what that says to the rest of youse, but I
sure as hell know what it says to me.

MACK   Dee, what's happening?

DEE   Oh for God's sake, it's just Merc, she's a flake, you
know Merc, she's ... a flake.

MACK   Dee, I don't understand, what's....

TOILANE I understand! I understand! I understand that I been
used! I been used in her sick fantasies and I been [*near
hysteria, makes terrible noise*] YOU LOVED ME! YOU
LOVED ME! YOU SAID THAT YOU LOVED ME! YOU
SAID you loved me and you asked me to – YOU SAID
THAT YOU WERE HORNIER THAN YOU'D EVER
BEEN, THAT YOU WERE WETTER FOR ME THAN....
[DEE *slaps him*]
You fuck ya fuckin cunt whore fuck. You're giving my baby
away! Because you don't want it and I'm not good enough, yo
throw me away like garbage and now my baby, now my BABE
MY....
[TOILANE *has been holding* DEE *by the arm. He throws her off at th
end of his speech.* MACK, *hearing this, realizing that it is genuine,
grabs his coat to go*]

DEE   MACKIE, FOR GOD'S SAKE, YOU DON'T BELIEVE
THE RAVINGS OF THIS....

MACK   He's not raving, he's real....

DEE   No he's not!

MACK   I KNOW YOU DEE, YOU FORGET!! WHAT GAME
ARE YOU PLAYING, EH? WHAT FUCKIN GAME?
[*he runs out*]

DEE   Maaaaaaaaaackieeeee!! [*she turns around and knocks
over her easel and a chair*] GET OUT OF MY HOUSE!!
OR I'LL LIGHT YOU ON FIRE I'LL LIGHT YOU ON
FIRE, GET OUT OF MY HOUSE.

PEGS [*grabs her*] Listen to me. You THINK what is right, I just want you to stop all this bull roar and THINK what is right. Can you do that?

DEE Get out.

PEGS We're going. We just wanted to drop by to inform ya that we will have our child. Whatever we have to do, wherever we have to go, we will have our child. Come on, son. And don't try and run away cause we'll find ya. You better believe we will.

[*They go*]

Act One, Scene Twenty-One

MERCY It's soo lovely outside, the ice on the trees is just ... you know, it's like the day that Mummy died, we'd been in that dark hospital room all day, holding her head trying to help her breathe, and then the breath gettin lighter and lighter until I thought we'd all stop breathing ... we'd all ... rise!! And then it stopped. I opened the door to the hall and a group of doctors were in a huddle and they suddenly laughed, roared like a big audience and I told them to shut up, my mother had just died, and then I walked down the back stairs and stepped out the door and the snow shone white, and these huge icy trees just ... showing ... themselves ... showing. And I was so startled ... to hear my own breath ... keep ... on ... [*pause*] I found this in your drawer. The locket, little silver heart, that Daddy gave you for your special club. 'Ich bin dein' ... what does that mean?

Act One, Scene Twenty-Two

RAYMOND *is looking through a book of medieval German poetry and he finds and reads the following poem, translating himself.*

RAYMOND Du bist mein
Ich bin dein
Des sollst du gewiss sein
Du bist verschlossen
In meinem Herzen
Verloren ist das Schlusselein
Du musst immer drinnen sein.
[*now, with understanding of the significance of the poem*]
... You are locked in my heart
The key is lost
You will always have to stay inside it....
For always.

Act Two, Scene Twenty-three

TOILANE's *place, very clean now. Mum has moved in temporarily. She comes in and lies down on the floor right away with her feet up.*

TOILANE [*after waiting for her to speak*] WELL?

PEGS This back is gonna be the death of me.

TOILANE What'd he say?

PEGS I got my arthritis puffin up my wrists. My stomach turnin into Mount St. Helens every five minutes. I don't know how I keep on keepin on.

TOILANE Mum, what'd he say?

PEGS BLOOD TESTS. IT ALL HINGES ON BLOOD TESTS.

TOILANE BLOOD TESTS?

PEGS And even that can't tell us for sure.

TOILANE But we know! I know it's mine, she told me!

PEGS Don't stand up in a court of law.

TOILANE Why not?

PEGS It's her word against yours. She charge you with assault, who they gonna believe?

TOILANE Her?

PEGS Yes her. Not only will they believe her but they could send you to jail for her. They could, unless we fight with everything we got. I'm serious Toi, this is no laughing matter.

TOILANE Oh. Fuck. Shit.

PEGS That's right.

TOILANE Jail?

PEGS That's what I said.

TOILANE Jail! Fuck! I'm not doin time again, I ... fuck. FUCK! Mum, maybe we should, like, maybe we should just like, forget it ... eh? I'm not goin down the river no way, I'm not going down the river again.

PEGS IS THAT YOUR BABY?

TOILANE Yes.

PEGS Are you gonna fight for it?

TOILANE I don't know.

PEGS Your dad was a quitter, that's how come he spent sixteen years in jail, are you a quitter too?

TOILANE No.

PEGS All evidence to the contrary, ARE YOU A QUITTER?

TOILANE NO!

PEGS Are you gonna let the high classes chew ya up and spit ya out? Are you gonna let them take your baby? My God I got to hate that class of people cleanin houses. I got to near throw up when I seen them comin; they used to talk to me like ya talk to a dog or a baby; 'Hello, Mrs. Creese, how ARE you today?' This one, Mrs. Morrin, I walk in, we're standin on her kitchen floor, so clean you could eat off it, and she says to me, she says: 'I don't know what was wrong with that last cleaning woman but she just couldn't get this floor clean!' and I'm thinkin 'get me outa here.' One day I'm talkin to her and she up and corrects my grammar. Well I turn around and says 'You think I don't know the correct grammar? I know it's "don't have any" but I say "don't got none." I CHOOSE "don't got none." I CHOOSE my grammar, cause I'd rather be dead; I'd rather be dead than be anything like you.' THEY HAVE US BELIEVIN WE CAN'T TALK, WE CAN'T DRESS, AND NOW THEY HAVE YOU BELIEVIN YOU DON'T HAVE A RIGHT TO YOUR CHILD! If you don't fight for your child you're worth even less than they think. Are you listening to me? Are you listening to me? Christ, they've got ya, don't they? They got ya so you don't care about your own blood!! Do ya?

TOILANE Yes.

PEGS Do ya?

TOILANE Yes!

PEGS Well tell em.

TOILANE I will.

PEGS Tell em.

TOILANE I – will – declare – war!

PEGS Yeah.

TOILANE I will ... I will ... I WILL DE ... CLARE ... WARRRR!!

[*The siren starts up now, the same siren that sounded when* DEE *was screaming earlier*]

I ... DE ... CLARE ... WARRRR!!

I ... DE ... CLARE ... WARRRR!!

I ... DE ... CLARE ... WARRRR!!

Act Two, Scene Twenty-four

MERCY *and* DEE *walking hand in hand, singing their childhood song.*

MERCY, DEE We are walking together, in the niice weatherrr
Ohhh what a lovelyyy daaaayy!! We are walking together, in the niice weatherrr
[*They laugh because they went off key*]

DEE Now you're not going to falter on the witness stand or walk away like that time at dinner?

MERCY No, I promised you, I promise.

DEE You swear on Mummy's grave?

MERCY Yes, I swear on Mummy's grave.

DEE Oh thank you!! YOU ARE A GOOD SISTER!!

MERCY Dierdre, do you love me?
[DEE *nods*]
Say 'I LOVE YOU MERCY' – say it.

DEE [*pause*] I love you Mercy.

MERCY More than anything on this earth?
[DEE *puts locket around* MERCY'*s neck*]

Act Two, Scene Twenty-five

TOILANE *and* PEGS *on their way to court. Dressed up.*
TOILANE *stops at a water fountain, and drinks.*

PEGS What the hell do you think you're doin.

TOILANE Having a drink of water, what do you think I'm doing?

PEGS Listen to me, have you ever seen a Chinese have a drink of cold water?

TOILANE Well ... no, I mean, I don't know.

PEGS Well you never have because they never would because they're smart and because they're smart they live to a hundred and five more often than not. Myrtle Chow told me never EVER to drink a drink of cold water no matter how thirsty you are. Blood goes straight to your stomach to warm ya up and it's game

161

over for your brain. Come to think of it, maybe that's
why you're as dumb as you are. Come on, we don't
want to be late for court for God's sake.

TOILANE I'm not dumb.

PEGS [*swings around*] DID YOU RAPE HER? DID YOU TRY
TO RAPE HER LIKE SHE SAYS YOU DONE?

TOILANE NOOOOOO!!! I TOLD YA NO NO NO NO NO NO
NO NO!!!

PEGS For Christ's sake, you'll get the cops on us. Toilane
camm down, camm down I SAID camm down okay.
It's not that I didn't believe you, it's just that when it
comes to young boys and sex, there's somethin so big
and dark that even a Mum don't know it so I JUST
HAD to ask you by surprise, that's what the cops do ...
always ask the accused by surprise, it always reveals
the truth. And you said no. So I believe you. I believe
you alright. Let's just hope to high heaven they do.
Gosh darn all those bloody B and E's and auto thefts
on your record from when we was living in
Burlington. I knew you was goin with a bad crowd
but I just wasn't sure how bad. DAMN THAT Kevin
Blanchard, DAMN him.

TOILANE It's not his fault. Jeez Mum, Kevin's got nothin to do
with....

PEGS Your past, my son, has everything, but everything to
do with your present. Every step of the way counts.
They don't miss a trick. Boy she thinks she got us over
a barrel, eh? Lying bitch. Her own sister won't even
back her up. She don't have a hope in hell today.

Act Two, Scene Twenty-six

MACK *addresses the audience.*

MACK When I first saw a girl naked I went into shock. I
started shaking, the other kids laughed but I was
scared, I was scared. I mean ... I knew girls were
different but I never imagined ... [*pause*] ... there used
to be these school dances, and we'd go, a bunch of us
and of course the really pretty girls were all taken, and

if there were any pretty girls left against the wall, you wouldn't dare ask them, I mean you wouldn't dare because if she turns you down you have to pass her in the halls every day for the rest of the year. NO WAY. So I used to ask this one ... I didn't even know her name but she'd always be there, with her friend, all covered in makeup, fat with a short skirt, big barrette in her hair to look prettier, and one time me and the guys had just been walking around all night, going to the washroom for a smoke, you know, the usual shit, and I was gettin sick of it, I wanted, you know, to touch a girl, so this slow dance came up and I tapped her on the shoulder. I didn't even say anything. She looked at me ... she had nice eyes ... and she came onto the dance floor, I held her so close, so close I swear I could have crushed her, so of course you know, I got an erection and it would be, well, up against her, she would just bury her head in my shoulder and we'd stay in this clutch ... we barely moved ... for the whole song. Then at the end of the song, I'd just turn around and walk away without looking at her. I never said hello to her in the halls. When my buddies asked me why I was dancing with that 'pig' I said she let me dry hump her on the dance floor. If I'm being punished, somehow, for that, now, I guess I deserve it. I guess I do.

Act Two, Scene Twenty-seven

Court corridor. PEGS *comes out after having talked to the lawyer.*

PEGS   Toi? Honey? ... we have to drop ... the suit.

TOILANE   What?

PEGS   The lawyer believes, is SURE, that with that sister backin her up now those girls will send you up for twenty years. Jail killed your father; it would most certainly kill you. I don't want to lose the both of youse.

TOILANE   But ... I thought you said

PEGS It doesn't matter what I said ... honey, they've brought us to our knees.

[MERCY *passes.* PEGS *grabs her*]

Hey

MERCY Please let me go.

PEGS We're human beings. We're not animals you know.

MERCY I didn't say you were an animal.

PEGS Why are you so AFRAID OF HER?

MERCY Because ... I love her. [*she wriggles free, runs away*]

Act Two, Scene Twenty-eight

TOILANE *is on the same ramp that he began the play with, apologizing to the judge so that he won't be charged with malicious prosecution. In court,* TOILANE *on stand.*

TOILANE And I ... apol – apulol-o-app – I'm sorry ... for makin up lies to the court ... I'm ... reall real real sorry and I'll never do it ... again ... [*whispers*] I'll never do it again.

Act Two, Scene Twenty-nine

Same day, after winning in court, DEE *and* MERCY *are in a victory dance. On the canvas is a grotesque painting of a nine-month-old fetus.*

ME WHOOOOO! WHOOO HOOOOOO!! Oh God. [*she flops down on the couch*] We won.

DEE Yes. [*pause*] We did the right thing didn't we? Don't you think?

MERCY [*takes off shoes*] I'm just glad they don't live here anymore. [*she prepares tea*]

DEE He couldn't have handled a child, I mean there's no way.

MERCY ... Do you want some tea?

DEE Merc? Don't you think?

[MERCY *goes out to make the tea*]

Uh!

MERCY What's that, a kick?

DEE BIG kick in the ribs. Hey, little one?! You getting restless? You want out, to the Johnsons? Hey Merc, don't you LOVE the Johnsons?

MERCY They seem nice.

DEE They're *fabulous*, fabulous people, Merc, the kid will thank me on its KNEES in twenty years. For sure! Oogh!

MERCY What's wrong, did something happen?

DEE [*checking under her skirt*] No no it's just ... a leak, I think a trickle – amniotic fluid, a ... oh, there's the mucous plug ... [*wraps it in kleenex*]

MERCY Does that mean ...

DEE No, no, I told you, it's just a leak, a trickle of water, it means there's a tear in one of the sacs, that's all, a little tear ... it could have torn it with its ... fingernail.

MERCY Are you sure we shouldn't go to hospital?

DEE No, I'm fine, I'd just like that tea I think.

ME Sure, sure, [*brings it*] here. Do you want something to eat?

[DEE *almost swoons*]

Dee? Are you alright?

DEE Ohh. Nooo! Ohhh! Oh my God, oh my God, a Lion a Lion, I can ... see – a – a – lion, a lion, breaking through the wall a lion roaring all the stones breaking, flying, roaring. Stop!

MERCY What do you mean, you see this in your mind?

DEE A lion! ... stop it! stop it!

MERCY Let's go to hospital, Dee, come on.

DEE AAAAAHH!!!

MERCY Let's go to hospital!

DEE No, no, no it's just lack of sleep ... it's lack of sleep, it's lack of sleep.

MERCY I know, I'll make you some hot milk, that'll make you feel better, let me make you some hot milk.

DEE It's lack of sleep. [*she lies down on the couch, shudders*]

[*Knock at the door.* MERCY *gets the door*]

PEGS We just ... my son just wanted to make an apology to youse, he feels bad for what he done, and....

MERCY Oh there's no need for that.

PEGS Oh, yes there is. We caused you people a lot of trouble and expense, and we want to apologize. Do you mind....

MERCY Well ...

DEE No, Merc, I'm going to bed I ... Really, there's no need for an apology, I....

PEGS Oh certainly there is, we'll just sit down and have a cup of tea with ya ... and ya see we want to be friends, we want to put all this mess behind us, and you know what I mean?

DEE It's just that I was about to go to bed, and

PEGS For God's sake give us this, girl, you had us evicted you made my son lie in court, for God's sake, let us be your friends. For his sake, not for mine, believe me if it was up to me....

DEE Okay, I'm sorry, please, have a seat. Mercy? Would you like to give these people some tea?

MERCY Okay. What do you take?

TOILANE No milk, two sugar please.

PEGS Just clear for me, thanks.

MERCY One clear, one double clear.

DEE So ... how do you like your new place?

PEGS Oh we like it fine. We'd been wanting to get outa here anyway, so really, you done us a favour.

DEE It wasn't anything to do with me whatever you may think, really, I hardly know the landlord.

PEGS Oh that's okay.

DEE Really!

PEGS I believe ya! That's a nice picture.

DEE Thank you, a friend did it.

PEGS Oh? What's it supposed to be?

DEE It's uh ... whatever you like....

PEGS Oh I get it.

MERCY Some biscuits?

PEGS Oh not for me, got to watch the old waistline.

MERCY You don't have a weight problem.

PEGS Oh that's very kind but I do. I weighed ninety pounds when I married Toi's father. [to DEE] Now you certainly don't have a weight problem ... how much you gained with the baby?

DEE Oh ... I don't know, I guess about twenty-five pounds. I don't really keep track.

PEGS No more than twenty, my doctor said. He said if I gained more than twenty he'd hang me.

DEE [*pause*] Did you?

PEGS Seventy-five pounds and I lived on chicken noodle soup. I'm serious.

[*As* PEGS *talks,* DEE *starts to go into mild labour. Of course, we have to speed things up: every half minute or so*]

MERCY Here's the tea ... double sugar for you and clear for you.

PEGS Thanks dear. Yes, as I say, he's going into retail management, what's the name of the store Toilane?

TOILANE Jones Work Warehouse, it's just like work clothes, sort of, and I'm just at the till, Ma, it's not management.

PEGS But darlin, nobody stays at the till certainly no son of mine, oh no you're far too smart to stay at the till.

MERCY I worked in retail for a while.

PEGS Did you now dear? Well did you get managerial?

MERCY No, no, I didn't.

PEGS Good tea, what kind is it? [*starts to notice* DEE *is in pain*]

DEE Darjeeling, I think, isn't it Merc?

PEGS That's Indian isn't it?

DEE I'm not sure.

PEGS You okay dear? You look a little uncomfortable.

DEE Oh, I'm fine, it's just ... the baby's foot sticks in my ribs ... I ... think I am gonna have to go lie down, actually.

PEGS Little tightness in the chest?

DEE Yuh, I just....

PEGS Here, lie down here, here, we'll sit in chairs, Toi can sit on the floor, we'll just finish our tea and we'll go.

DEE Really I

PEGS There, there, just lie yourself down, I was a RNA I know what I'm talking about a little company's not gonna kill you.

DEE [*lies down*] Okay, just a few minutes, though.

PEGS Comfy now? You'll be okay. Well! This is like a reunion after so long! Eh? Just a bunch of friends, after all that's happened? Who would thought it ... Toilane knows he mighta made a mistake ... I do, however, think it would be a nice gesture if you ... admit, just for me bein his mum, that my son did not assault you.

DEE Oh listen, if I thought you were going to....

PEGS No no no now don't get het up. I just want you to tell me whether or not my son assaulted you.

DEE I withdrew the charge. What does it matter.

PEGS It matters to me, I'm his mother.

DEE He knows the truth.

PEGS I think we all know the truth.

DEE Would you please leave?

PEGS No. I'm enjoying the reunion; and after what you done to us I think we gotta right ...

[DEE *reaches for phone*]

Toi.

[TOILANE *cuts the phone.* DEE *gets up*]

DEE What is this?

[MERCY *runs to door.* TOILANE *blocks the door*]

PEGS We want ... to be treated ... *hospitable* by you! We want the respect ... we deserve! Now sit down and talk nice.

[*They sit down nervously.* DEE's *waters break*]

DEE AGHHHHH.

PEGS Your waters!

MERCY Deedee are you okay?

DEE It's nothing, nothing.

PEGS Nothing! My dear your waters broke!

MERCY I really think we ought to be going. Dee I'll get your coat.

PEGS YOU'RE NOT GOING ANYWHERE TILL WE'VE HAD OUR VISIT. NOW SIT DOWN.

MERCY You're crazy. YOU'RE A CRAZY LADY!

PEGS You try to leave and my son will do whatever he has to do to stop you. So sit down.

MERCY Just ... a short visit, then, please?

PEGS I WANT MY REUNION!

[DEE *contracts, bad labour pain throughout this speech*]

Huh, speakin of reunions, I got a story. We had our high school reunion last year and of course I didn't want to go, I'd got so old, fat, you know, but my girlfriend, Janis, she said, oh come on, we're all old and fat, we'll have a ball, get out the rum and cokes, and the taco chips ... play a little bingo, have a blast! So finally I thought, oh alright, so I trudged on over with Janis, and I had a pretty good time, and I was sittin at a table havin a pie and coffee with a few girls when one of em says, well she says, 'I've had such a nice time, but I just wish to heaven that Peggy Lane had come,' Lane's my maiden name, 'she's always such a laugh.' Well I musta turned three shades a red, I could hardly speak but I did, like a fool, I turned to her and I said, 'But Marjorie, here I am, I'm Peggy! Didn't you see me?' Well then SHE turned three shades of red and she SAID, 'Well, yes, I did, but I wouldn't have known you ... your FACE!' My face, had got so ... it's true I guess, I don't look nothing like my wedding pictures. Toi don't believe me when I tell him how pretty I was.

TOILANE Yes I do.

PEGS Isn't that a funny one? You okay, dear? Looks like you're gonna have a baby in a day or so! Toi? I guess we'd better be goin. [PEGS *gets up,* TOILANE *is still*] Toi?

TOILANE I don't want to go.

PEGS Toi, the lady is going to have a baby, good God

TOILANE I want ... my baby.

PEGS But Toi, the courts ruled.

TOILANE I don't care what the courts ruled. I want my baby.

PEGS Well you can have another one, there are plenty of girls out there.

TOILANE I want my baby with the woman I love.

PEGS Toi, you don't love her you had a silly crush, now

TOILANE I love her and she loves me. I love you. You love me and you are going to have my baby and I ... want it. I want to take care of it. Mum, you know you said if there was anything I really needed you would be there for me, you'd help me out.

PEGS Toi.

TOILANE You said to trust you, you said you'd come through, are you gonna help me?

PEGS Help you what?

TOILANE Deliver the baby.

PEGS Toi for God's sake, what if there's complications?

TOILANE What?

PEGS If that baby won't come out, she might have to have a Caesarian you know, be cut out.

TOILANE Well you done that, you done them things you said, when you worked in the hospital.

PEGS   Toi, this is ... against the law, this is....
       [DEE *is about to vomit*]
       Do you need to throw up dear? [*she gets something*]
       Here, if you want to throw up.
       [DEE *does*]
DEE   I want to go to hospital, I want....
TOILANE   I WANT MY CHILD. I'M GONNA HAVE MY
       CHILD.
DEE   You can't do this, this is sick, this is....
PEGS   My son wants his child and he got a right and you
       know he does. Now nobody's gonna hurt you. We're
       just gonna take what is rightfully ours.
DEE   Just for Christ's sake, can't you just leave.
       MERCEEEEE!!
       [MERCY *stands up. Stands on her tippytoes. Lifts her
       hands high in the air. Eyes wide, turns around and walks
       out*]
TOILANE   Hey.
PEGS   It's okay, let her go.
TOILANE   But what if she drops a dime, Ma?
PEGS   She won't.
TOILANE   She won't?
PEGS   She won't.
DEE   Oh no oh nooo it's coming again it's coming again the
       big lion is comiing down to crush me to crush me oh
       no oh no ohhh I can't stand it I can't stand it
       uhhhhhhhh Mackie, Mackie, please, please, take me to
       hospital, I think I'm gonna die, I really think I'm gonna
       die.
PEGS   That's what they all say dear, the schoolyards are full.
TOILANE   I'm your husband now. I'll help ya through it.
DEE   Oh God, oh God, I must be in hell, that's what it is. I
       died and I'm in hell, or I know! It's a dream, that's
       what it is, a terrible nightmare, oh God, oh
       AGHHHHH. LET ME WAKE UP PLEASE LET ME
       WAKE UP.
PEGS   [*to* TOILANE] I think it's time we brought her into the
       bedroom, Toi, she'll be more comfortable there.
DEE   NOOOOO!!!
       [TOILANE *helps* DEE *into the bedroom*]

[*to* TOILANE] You ... you won't let me die will you?
Will you?

TOILANE I love you, Dee, I'd never let you die.
[DEE, *crying, collapses into his arms*]

Act Two, Scene Thirty

This could be a dream. MERCY, *stunned in courtyard.*
RAYMOND *walks by. She is just staring.*

RAYMOND [*after looking several times*] Excuse me, excuse me but
your name wouldn't happen to be ... Mercia ... would
it?

MERCY Yes. Who are you?

RAYMOND Raymond. Raymond Brisson from ... I used to drive
you to school when you were ... a schoolgirl ... in
Montreal ... you were about fifteen, I believe – St.
Francis.

MERCY Raymond.

RAYMOND Yes, that's right – Raymond ... How strange to see you
here, do you live ... in one of these apartments?

MERCY Yes. Do you?

RAYMOND Well I keep a small flat here ... you see I teach here
twice a week, so I go back and forth from the country.

MERCY It's ... funny to see you, like seeing the house I grew up
in with different people living in it, it's funny.

RAYMOND Yes, it's that way seeing you too. As if – a – light –
switched.

MERCY Oh Raymond, I love the way you touched me.

RAYMOND [*blushes deeply*] ... Are you alright? You seem to be....

MERCY What, what do I seem?

RAYMOND Well, it looks as if you've had a bit of a shock.

MERCY It's just that I see you, and all I want, all I really want is
for you to touch me again.

RAYMOND It's lovely to see you.

MERCY Oh Raymond, I've had so many ... dreams about you,
you know nobody's touched me in the same ... way,
made the honey – pour –

RAYMOND   Say, would you like a cup of tea, why don't you come
up to my flat and I'll get you a cup of tea and a – a –
biscuit.

MERCY   Yeah, I'd like to come up to your flat, I'll come up to
your flat and have a nice cup of tea and then I'm going
to take off my clothes and I'm going to spread my legs
and you're going to ... make love to me. We never
went all the way, you know, in the car, we only ever
did everything but.

RAYMOND   [*clearly aroused*] Well, let's just see about that tea first
of all and sitting you down....

MERCY   I dreamed about you all the time.
[RAYMOND *and* MERCY *hold position*]

Act Two, Scene Thirty-one

TOILANE *and* PEGS *and baby on a bus in the night.*
TOILANE *goes to light a cigarette.*

PEGS   No smokin with the baby, Toi, you should know that!

TOILANE   Oh right. How is she?

PEGS   Oh Tracy Meg is just fine, sleepin like a baby.

TOILANE   Ever cute! You sure you brought enough formula?

PEGS   I brought you up didn't I? Trust me for God's sake.

TOILANE   I do, I do, I'm just ... nervous, you know. What if they
catch up with us? [*pause*] Ma, do you think she's okay?

PEGS   Who?

TOILANE   Deedree.

PEGS   Sure she's okay. She never wanted a baby and now
she doesn't have one.

TOILANE   I love her though Mum you know, I still love her.

PEGS   Don't be a sap.

TOILANE   I'll love her till the day I die! Hey. Do you think she
looks like me?

PEGS   I think she looks like your father, if you want to know
the truth.

TOILANE   But she looks like our side, like, you can definitely see
it's mine.

PEGS   Oh no question about it, the minute I saw her.

TOILANE It's like there's a well, you know and when I seen her, Tracy? Something pumped that water up and it filled my whole head, you know, it filled my whole head!

Act Two, Scene Thirty-two

Waiting room. MERCY *and* MACK.

MERCY But I betrayed her, I betrayed my own sister. I thought, you know, I thought it was the right thing. I wanted to do the right thing for once in my life. I'm sorry you know but I'm not at the same time. Do you know what I mean? I mean I'm sorry but I'm not sorry I'm not I'm sorry I'm not I'm sorry I'm not I'm not I'm sorry.
[*They go into the hospital room.* DEE *is in bed, breasts bandaged. She wakes up*]

DEE Mercy.
[*She reaches for her.* MERCY *goes and hugs* DEE]
Mercy. Where's the baby?

MERCY Dee, she's ... she's in the nursery. She's in the nursery with the other babies. She's fine.

DEE A girl? She's a girl?

MERCY Yes, a little girl.

DEE And they didn't get her? Him and his mother, they didn't get her?

MERCY No Dee, they left. They left and we went to the hospital and you had the baby. You just had a very rough time. You had a very rough birth.

DEE Then it was a dream? You mean it was a dream? But I was so sure it was real, no it couldn't have been a dream, you're lying to me, you're lying....

MERCY Mackie –

DEE You're lying, where's my baby, where's my....

MACK She's here, I told you Dee. She's ... okay, really.

DEE She is? She is?

MACK The baby is just fine. The nurses are taking care of her in the nursery – she's in the nursery.

DEE But I was sure that it wasn't a dream. Mackie? Mackie?

MACK You're okay Dee, you're gonna be okay.

DEE Are you gonna stay with me? You aren't going to leave?

MACK No, I'm not going to leave.

DEE Cause, cause I want to keep our baby now, Mack, I want to keep her. The Johnsons aren't here, are they, get them away, get them away.

MACK I just think you ought to get some rest now Deirdre.

DEE But I want to see my baby, show me my baby, show me my baby. My God, you're on fire, your eyes are on fire. Your eyes are on fire!
[MACK *interjects throughout the speech with 'Shh' and 'No, no'*]
Mercy, Mercy, your face your face is burning, burning burning, white. I want to talk to my mother. I want to talk to my mother.

MERCY But Dee, Mummy's dead, she's dead.

MACK DEE.

DEE I know, I know she's dead, I know she's dead but I want to talk to her, I want to ... talk to her, I want ... to tell her that I'm ... sorry! I want to say I'm sorrry!! I'm sorrry!! I'm sorrrry!! I'm sorrrry!!

Act Two, Scene Thirty-three

RAYMOND *speaking to* MERCY, *but it doesn't matter if she is on stage or not. He should NOT be speaking directly to her.*

RAYMOND I dreamed about you too, you know, several times a year every time the season changed. Swimming, swimming in cold blue water, clear; striped fish and dark, inky seals jumping around us, and I turn, and look at you and your eyes, your eyes are toooo ... blue.... And then I'd wake up, look out the window and see the first snowfall, or the leaves had turned ... overnight....

Act Two, Scene Thirty-four

PEGS *and* TOILANE *in hotel room. Light flashing outside.*

TOILANE Sudbury on a Saturday night eh?

PEGS Sssshh shhh. I think she's down.

TOILANE [*sits down*] Mum.

PEGS Yuh.

TOILANE I wanted to tell you ... that ... like ... I wanted to apologize.

PEGS What for?

TOILANE For that time ... when I was in grade four that time, and ... we were having the goodbye thing ... party or something for Mrs. Lamb.

PEGS She was your favourite teacher.

TOILANE And you came to get me just when I's gonna give my present to her, I was just giving it to her and there you were and I was so embarrassed you looked so ... bright or something, too bright or too big ... so ... I said for you to get out. I said, 'Get out of here mother,' and you did, you ran, crying down the hill, and broke your high heel. I felt so bad about that high heel, about you breakin it on that hill cause of me. Okay.

PEGS It was damn stupid of me, I knew how much that teacher meant to you, I shouldn't have come.

TOILANE Mum, how come she breathes so fast?

PEGS Babies do, they breathe fast ... look at her little face, will ya?

TOILANE Mum? What ... do you think she's dreamin? Do you think she's dreamin?

PEGS I don't know. Little rose.

TOILANE Little rose.

PEGS Ohhhh. Boy. I'm gonna have to sit down I'm not feelin too good.

TOILANE What's the matter?

[PEGS *should not be sitting on bed, but on a chair beside the bed*]

PEGS I think it was that sandwich, the Toasted Western, I think it musta been bad.

TOILANE Yah? What ... is it your stomach or

PEGS No, my head, it feels like my head's on fire, like white....

Act Two, Scene Thirty-five

DEE *opens a door. A light blinds the audience. She walks forward on the ramp towards the audience. The audience, to her, is the nursery. She is looking for her baby. She feels purified – through birth – and also through understanding her self-hatred, her guilt about her mother – she is now able to love after having grappled with her 'shadow' or 'animal.' She is infused with this love. She sees the baby somewhere in the audience. (Not picking out an individual, of course.)*

DEE Ohhhh! Which ... one are you, baby? Which ... Oh! I see you! I see you now! Oh! You are so ... beautiful. Yes! Yes! I want you baby I want you forever because I ... love you. I LOVE you. Oh! Oh! Your eyes are opening ... Hello! Hello! Hello! Hello!

Act Two, Scene Thirty-six

We cross-fade to TOILANE. *In the hotel room, hotel light still flashing.* PEGS *passed out or maybe dead in chair.* TOILANE *stands there, holding the baby, bewildered.*

TOILANE Mum??